dream
machines
cars

dream
machines
cars

jonathan wood

p

Page 1: The spirit of the E-Type is evoked by Jaguar's XKR 100 coupé of 2001 created to commemorate the centenary of the company's founder, William Lyons.

Page 2: Jaguar's greatest, the fabulous E-Type, derived from the Le Mans-winning D-Type. This is a 3.8 litre car of 1962.

Page 3: The immensely impressive Aston Martin Vanquish – Britain's very own Ferrari-chaser.

Above: Ferrari's stylish 550 Barchetta Pininfarina, unveiled at the 2000 Paris Motor Show.

Opposite: The power unit of Porsche's fastest ever road car, the mighty GT2.

This is a Parragon Book

First published in 2002

Parragon
Queen Street House
4 Queen Street
Bath BA1 1HE, UK

Copyright © Parragon 2002

Designed, produced and packaged by
Stonecastle Graphics Limited

Text by Jonathan Wood
Edited by Philip de Ste. Croix
Designed by Paul Turner and Sue Pressley

ISBN 0-75257-457-4

Printed in China

Photographic credits:
All photographs © Neill Bruce's Automobile Photolibrary, with the exception of the following, which are manufacturers' press pictures supplied from the Peter Roberts Collection c/o Neill Bruce:
page 1; page 3; page 4; page 57 *centre right*: page 63 *top*; page 63 *centre left*; page 67 *top left*; page 75 *top*; page 75 *centre*; pages 76-77; pages 78-79; pages 80-81; pages 82-83; pages 84-85; page 88; page 89 *top right*; pages 90-91; pages 94-95.

Other pictures by:
Ian Dawson © Neill Bruce's Automobile Photolibrary: page 58 *below*; page 59 *below*.
Geoffrey Goddard © Neill Bruce's Automobile Photolibrary: page 32; page 33 *below*; page 56 *centre left*; page 57.
Stefan Lüscher © Neill Bruce's Automobile Photolibrary: page 5; page 7 *top*; page 67 *top right*; page 67 *centre*; page 86 *below*; page 87; pages 92-93.

Neill Bruce is grateful to Bonhams & Brooks, Nigel Dawes and Duncan Hamilton Ltd for making many of the cars available for photography.

Please note: Unless otherwise stated, the performance figures of the cars featured in this book refer to the speeds recorded at the time of the model's introduction.

Contents

We've all done it. We rapturously admire a special car in the street as its roars or prowls past; we see it at a motor show, in a car magazine or on our television and we start to dream. Almost certainly the model in question is beyond the reach of our pockets but its fabulous styling and breathtaking performance draw us like a magnet. Such cars possess an indefinable magic – you can't pin it down but it's definitely there!

Fortunately for dreamers like us the post-war years have seen the emergence of a handful of motor manufacturers who seem unable to produce anything but dream machines. Ferrari has only been building cars since 1947, and nearly every model, almost invariably enhanced by a Pininfarina body of mouth-watering innovation and elegance, would qualify for such an accolade.

A number of car makers have attempted to challenge Ferrari's pre-eminence but, of these, only Lamborghini has come close to securing this elusive goal, even if it has had no less than five owners since its birth in 1963. This is the company that has produced the likes of the innovative mid-engined Miura and the outrageous, wildly impractical Countach.

Unlike Ferrari, Lamborghini has no racing pedigree but Porsche, which produced its first car in 1948, possesses this in abundance. The 356,

the onset of the muscle car era in America, a survives to this day. The 'Ray's arrival announced building since 1953 and one which, happily, of a model line that General Motors had been Chevrolet Corvette Sting Ray, a 1963 manifestation This was a model that in its turn inspired the E-Type, for many the ultimate dream car. sports racing D-Type gave birth, in 1961, to the than five occasions in the 1950s, its legendary Winner of the Le Mans 24 hour race on no less successful when, in 1989, it purchased Jaguar. by Fiat. But the American car company was more rebuffed and Ferrari has, since 1969, been owned 1987, attempted to acquire Ferrari. The bid was Back in 1962 Ford, which bought Aston Martin in

Le Mans-winning heritage

horse firmly in its sights. acclaimed Vanquish which has Ferrari's prancing Martin has just launched the fabulous and Modena. With a distinguished racing history, Aston spirit of the blood red berlinettas (coupés) from Martin – its DB2 of 1950 was conceived in the If Ferrari has a British equivalent, it is Aston

evergreen 911 successor espouses to this day. engine, so establishing a precedent that its seemingly powered by a rear-mounted horizontally opposed based on the Porsche-designed VW Beetle, was

Below: A legend is born with America's first sports car of the post-war years. This is a Chevrolet Corvette, a model line that endures to this day and is still bodied in glass-fibre. Unusually the hood is raised on this 1955 example. When not in use, it was stored in a well concealed beneath a hinged cover behind the seats.

stampede that began in 1964 with the Pontiac GTO and lead to the likes of the bewinged Plymouth Road Runner Superbird of 1970. Whether this should be considered a dream car or a nightmare only the beholder can decide…

America is, of course, the home of the big, slow-revving but powerful V8 engine which European car makers have recognized as an accessible and economical method of ensuring a performance formula. This has resulted in such sensational and potent street machines as the Anglo/American AC Cobra, the South London-born Allard, France's Facel Vega and the Iso Grifo from Milan.

The size and prosperity of the US market has meant that, in recent years, the German Mercedes-Benz and BMW companies have established car factories there. Both have excellent track records of producing memorable models; Mercedes' gullwing-doored 300SL coupé of 1954 is perhaps the quintessential dream car. BMW has produced generations of finely engineered sports saloons, and this enviable tradition is maintained in its present state-of-the-art Z8 sports car.

BMW purchased Rolls-Royce in 1998 while its Bentley stablemate was acquired in the same year by Volkswagen. Like Jaguar, Bentley possesses an impressive Le Mans racing record although its five victories there occurred long ago between 1924 and 1930. This competitive pedigree was revived in the 1950s by the high-speed Continental coupé, a creation that Bentley's Rolls-Royce parent successfully revived in 1991.

Like most of Britain's surviving motoring industry, Bentley is now in foreign hands and the same goes for Lotus which was acquired by the Malaysian Proton concern in 1996. A company that produced its first sports car in 1951, Lotus's models have been at the cutting edge of engineering

technology ever since. The hand-built, ultra-conservative Morgan, which has been in the ownership of its founding family since 1910, offers a complete contrast. Morgan's current Aero 8 manages to combine long-nurtured traditional engineering with 21st-century technology.

TVR, by contrast, is a mere stripling, having marketed its first kit cars with glass-fibre bodies in 1954. Owned since 1982 by Peter Wheeler, who also styles his own products, today TVR's distinctive sports cars enliven our highways in a way that their predecessors never did. And TVR's mighty Cerbera Speed 12 is hoping to challenge the McLaren F1 as the world's fastest production car.

Built between 1994 and 1997, McLaren's F1 coupé embraced costly and sophisticated Formula 1 technology. It was capable of 240mph (386km/h) and had sensational acceleration to match. Costing £540,000 apiece, just 100 were sold to lucky owners the world over. In other words the F1 possesses all the attributes of the dream car – it's fabulous but ultimately unobtainable!

Above: BMW's Z8 of 2000, with lines inspired by the 507 roadster of the 1950s, is capable of 155mph (249km/h). Built around an aluminium space-frame, the 8 is not only light, its body structure sets new standards for rigidity.

Below left: The mid-engined McLaren F1 of 1993 was based on racing technology and was capable of 240mph (386km/h). Only able to seat three occupants, access is made much easier by these distinctive upward-opening doors.

Metrication inches forward

Because the automobile is a European invention, ever since its arrival in 1886 the motor industry has measured the cubic capacity and internal dimensions of its engines in the metric measurements of cubic centimetres, litres and millimetres. But across the Atlantic, America's car makers instead adopted inches and cubic inches, which is why the sizes of the engines of the American cars in this book are quoted in cubic inches (cid). However, in recent years the increasing globalization of the industry has seen a gradual switch by US motor manufacturers to metric measurements, even if cubic capacity is now rendered by them in *liters* rather than cubic centimetres (cc).

Jaguar XK120

The first of Jaguar's fabled XK sports car line, the 120 was so named because it could attain 120mph (193km/h), an unprecedented speed for a production model of its day. Announced at the 1948 London Motor Show, the line was destined to survive until 1961 when the XK150 made way for the sensational E-Type.

The 120's powerful performance came courtesy of a 3.4 litre, twin-overhead-camshaft, six-cylinder engine, the legendary XK unit, that had been conceived during the war to power the company's new 100mph (161km/h) Mark VII saloon. This, paradoxically, appeared in 1950, after the open two-seater sports car.

Manufactured for export

William Lyons, Jaguar's accomplished chairman who also styled his company's products, ensured that his new model had the looks to match its performance. It was conceived at a time when the British government was directing the country's

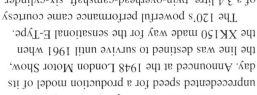

Top speed 120mph 193km/h

motor manufacturers to export their products overseas and the overwhelming majority of the Coventry-built XK120s were produced in left-hand-drive form for the American market.

Based on the chassis of the simultaneously announced Mark V saloon, the public was astounded by the new Jaguar's much publicized top speed. Lyons confounded his critics by carefully preparing a mildly streamlined test car which, in 1949, attained 132mph (212km/h) on the Jabbeke motorway in Belgium.

Demand for the 120 was intense. After the first 240 cars, which used aluminium bodywork, had been completed, steel panels replaced the aluminium – a change that modestly increased the model's weight.

The new XK engine undeniably proved its worth. While the twin-cam concept had a pre-war reputation for unreliability, the new Jaguar unit was durable and dependable, to the extent that it remained in production until 1992.

Below: This 1949 XK120 is a rare aluminium-bodied example. Most of these are identifiable by the curved windscreen pillars and accompanying large rubber grommets; the rest of the outward features are shared with the steel-bodied cars. Although this is a right-hand-drive version, the vast majority of 120s were left hookers destined for the American market.

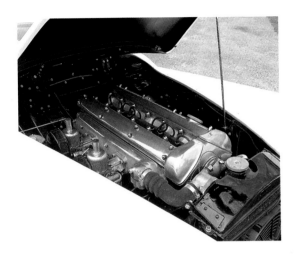

Left: How it achieved 120mph (193km/h): the 120's legendary twin-overhead-camshaft XK engine. The absence of studs on the front of the cam covers indicates an early car.

Left below: Most 120s had a black steering wheel, but white was occasionally offered during the XK150 production run. The hood was stored behind the seats when not in use.

Below: This fine XK120 fixed-head coupé in rallying guise has optional wire wheels in place of the usual discs and bonnet straps. Unlike the roadster, this possessed a walnut dash and door cappings, courtesy of Jaguar's saloon line.

Enter the drophead coupé

In 1951 the XK120 roadster was joined by a drophead coupé version. This was not only stylistically successful but it also had an enhanced interior with walnut veneer replacing the open car's leathercloth-covered instrument panel.

A Special Equipment package was offered for both versions from 1952 and this included high lift camshafts, a lightened flywheel, twin exhaust pipes and handsome centre-lock wire wheels which replaced the original discs. These ministrations added 20bhp to the 160bhp the XK unit developed in 1948.

The final variation on the XK120 theme was a drophead coupé which appeared in 1953. This combined the comfort of the fixed head coupé with the fresh air of an open car. Mechanically there was little to choose between all three models although the later versions used a quieter Salisbury rear axle.

XK 120 production ceased in the autumn of 1954. By then, Jaguar had established itself as one of the world's leading sports car manufacturers.

Specification	Jaguar XK120
Engine location	Front, in-line
Configuration	Six-cylinder
Bore and stroke	83 x 106mm
Capacity	3442cc
Valve operation	Twin overhead camshafts
Horsepower	160bhp @ 5000rpm
Transmission	Manual four-speed
Drive	Rear
Chassis	Box section
Suspension – front	Wishbone and torsion bar
Suspension – rear	Half-elliptic spring
Brakes	Drum
Top speed	120mph (193km/h)
Acceleration	0-60mph (96km/h): 12 seconds

Ferrari 166 Inter

Above: One of a handful of pillarless coupés that Touring built on the 166 chassis, each differing slightly from one another. Even though produced in Italy, these early Ferraris are right-hand-drive cars.

Right: A Spyder Corsa competition version of the 166 with an open two-seater body for sports racing events, but with the minimum of weather equipment. Note the length of the bonnet which concealed a V12 engine, a feature of the marque that still endures.

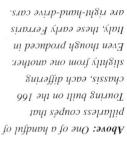

Top speed 100mph 161km/h

The 166 has the distinction of being Enzo Ferrari's first road car, but it was not his first model, that accolade being accorded to the competition-honed Type 125 of 1947. Unusually for the day Ferrari opted for a V12 engine and the 2 litre, 60 degree unit which had a single overhead camshaft per bank was designed for him by Gioacchino Colombo, creator of Alfa Romeo's famous Alfetta racing car of 1938.

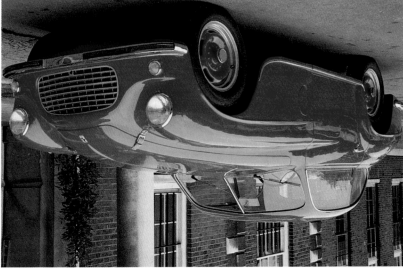

Romeo's famous Alfetta racing car of 1938.

Enzo Ferrari

Enzo Ferrari had managed Alfa Romeo's racing team in the 1930s, and so (not surprisingly) he adopted a similar approach to competition when he established a marque under his own name. During 1947 and 1948 all the cars produced at the Maranello works were either campaigned by the factory or by their prosperous owners.

Introduced in competition-proven 166 Sport form in 1947, the 166 Inter was a touring Ferrari, if that is not a contradiction in terms. Announced at the 1948 Turin Motor Show, the first two examples were fitted with coupé bodies by the respected Carrozzeria Touring concern and built to its superleggera (super light) principles featuring a sub-structure of small diameter tubes.

The closed car conjured up echoes of the body that Touring had already produced for Alfa Romeo; the finely proportioned, austere open version with its distinctive sculptured front was named the barchetta (little boat) and it was widely imitated.

The 166's engine was mounted in an oval tubular chassis enhanced by transverse leaf front suspension although the live axle was sprung with conventional half-elliptic rear springs. A five-speed gearbox with synchromesh on third and top gears was employed.

Specification	**Ferrari** 166 Inter
Engine location	Front, in-line
Configuration	V12
Bore and stroke	60 x 58mm
Capacity	1995cc
Valve operation	Single overhead camshaft per bank
Horsepower	110/115bhp @ 6000rpm
Transmission	Manual five-speed
Drive	Rear
Chassis	Oval tubular
Suspension – front	Wishbones and transverse leaf spring
Suspension – rear	Half-elliptic spring
Brakes	Drum
Top speed	100mph (161km/h)
Acceleration	N/A

At that time Ferrari only sold his cars in chassis form – they were then bodied in response to a specific customer or dealer order. This is why no two 166s are exactly alike! In all Touring created the bodies for some five cars, but other examples were the work of a variety of talented Italian coachbuilders, namely Stablimenti Farina, Vignale, Bertone, Allemano and Ghia.

Three prestigious road race wins

Capable of a reliable and sustainable 100mph (161km/h), in 1949 Ferrari 166s won the world's three most prestigious road races, namely the Mille Miglia, the Targa Florio and Le Mans. The 24 hour race in 1949 was the first to be held since the end of the Second World War, and Chinetti and Selsdon averaged 82.27mph (132.4km/h). Ferrari would go on to take the chequered flag at the Sarthe circuit on no less than nine occasions.

Above left: Although Ferrari maintained that he chose a V12 engine because of its use by Packard in 1915, it was a configuration employed in Mercedes-Benz and Alfa Romeo racing cars in the immediate pre-war years.

Left: The no-frills barchetta two-seater created for the 166MM chassis by Touring. The company's famous Superleggera badge can be seen on the front right-hand side of the bonnet with the nearby cold air intake serving the engine's carburettors.

Below left: The barchetta's cockpit with the distinctive leather beading around its edge readily apparent, as is Ferrari's prancing horse motif on the steering wheel boss. Unusually for the day, the 166 was fitted with a five-speed gearbox.

In two years about 39 examples of the 166 were produced, three Sports and 36 Inters. Although the 166 was listed into 1953, it had been replaced the previous year by the 2.5 litre 212. Ferrari was on his way!

Allard J2

Below: *Stripped for action: a J2X destined for the American market and fitted with aero screens rather than the usual full-width windscreen. The longer nose concealed the coil springs that had been exposed on the J2.*

**Top speed
130mph**
209km/h

Sydney Allard had campaigned Ford V8-based specials in pre-war days and in 1938 he began limited production of such cars at his garage in the south London suburb of Clapham. Work stopped during the Second World War but manufacture resumed in 1946. Allard offered the chunky no-frills K1 open two-seater with its distinctive waterfall-style cowled radiator. The accent was on simplicity and a good power-to-weight ratio. Allard used a straightforward chassis and a simple but effective divided independent front suspension axle although he retained Ford's crude Model T-inspired transverse leaf springing. The three-speed gearboxes came from the same source.

Monte Carlo Rally

The robust 3.6 litre side-valve V8 engine provided both reliability and acceleration and the K1 was joined by L and M1 four-seaters, while Sydney Allard himself won the 1952 Monte Carlo Rally in the P1 saloon version.

But the sports-racing J2 of 1949 saw a return to first principles. The open two-seater body did away with doors and was removable: it was even starker than its predecessors and came complete with cycle wings. It was ideal transport for the enthusiast who wanted to drive to the racetrack and then compete there. The J2's mechanicals differed from the earlier models with the use of a de Dion rear axle and all-round coil springs.

Even when Ford V8-powered, with a 4.4 litre Mercury ohv conversion, the J2 was capable of over 100mph (161km/h), but when one of the new generation of American V8s was installed, then the Allard really went motoring. These engines, it should be said, were usually fitted in those cars sold on the US market, because import restrictions prevented the Allard company from spending precious dollars on the purchase of new units.

However, the firm was able to acquire a few engines for experimental purpose and the prototype 331cid (5.4 litre) Cadillac-engined J2 with 160bhp on tap was capable of a spirited 130mph (209km/h), no less than 100mph (161km/h) in second gear and 80mph (129km/h) in first cog!

Specification	**Allard** J2 (Cadillac engine)
Engine location	Front, in-line
Configuration	V8
Bore and stroke	3.81 x 3.63in (97 x 92mm)
Capacity	331cid (5.4 litres)
Valve operation	Pushrod
Horsepower	160bhp @ 4000rpm
Transmission	Manual three-speed
Drive	Rear
Chassis	Box section
Suspension – front	Divided beam and coil spring
Suspension – rear	De Dion axle and coil spring
Brakes	Drum
Top speed	130mph (209km/h)
Acceleration	0-60mph (96km/h): 7 seconds

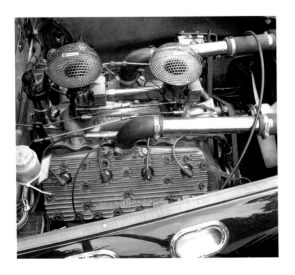

With such acceleration it could pull away from a Jaguar XK120. American enthusiasts also delighted in fitting alternative Oldsmobile or Chrysler V8s. This latter unit, also of 331cid, was a feature of the revised J2X for the 1952 season. This outwardly resembled its predecessor although it had a longer nose section because the engine was mounted 7in (178mm) further forward to allow more room for the occupants.

Built until 1952, the X was succeeded by the Cadillac-engined JR of 1953, the last of the line. Its aerodynamic body was in stark contrast to the functional appeal of its predecessor. In all 187 J Series cars were built, 99 J2s, 83 J2Xs and just five JRs. By 1960 the Allard was no more.

Above: A J2 showing its original windscreen and distinctive triangulated side pieces in place. The spare wheel could be fitted on either side of the body.

Left: A J2 fitted with a 3.6 litre British-built Ford V8. Although a side-valve unit, aluminium cylinder heads were added to extract 90bhp rather than the usual 85.

Aston Martin DB2

Top speed
118mph
190km/h

The famous Aston Martin marque was effectively reborn with the appearance, in April 1950, of the DB2. Named after David Brown, the company's owner since 1947, the model was destined to survive until 1959.

It represented the union of Aston Martin with the Lagonda make that Brown had acquired in 1947. The chassis, of square section tubes, came courtesy of a 1939 Aston Martin prototype saloon named the Atom, while the 2.6 litre, 100bhp, twin-overhead-camshaft, six-cylinder engine was the work of W.O. Bentley, no less. It had been designed to power the post-war Lagonda saloon car line which Brown also perpetuated.

However, his first Aston Martin was the 2 litre Super Sports of 1948, retrospectively dubbed the DB1. This, like the pre-war cars, was an open model and used the Atom's chassis and ohv engine. But it was an expensive concept and only 15 were sold. Production ceased in 1950.

It was replaced in that year by the DB2 which boasted closed coachwork in the manner of the latest sporting *gran turismos* from Italy. The work of talented Lagonda stylist, Frank Feeley, it was every inch a thoroughbred and performed as well as it looked. Top speed was in the region of 110mph (177Km/h), but later in 1950 a more powerful 116bhp Vantage version appeared and a drophead coupé body was also introduced.

Right: Unusually, the entire front end of the DB2 hinged forward to permit access to the Bentley-designed twin-overhead-camshaft engine and independent front suspension.

Below: The DB2 in its original form with body lines inspired by the Italian berlinettas of the day. At this stage only two occupants could be accommodated.

Arrival of the new DB2/4

The 1954 season saw the arrival of the DB2/4 which turned the mainstream coupé into an occasional four-seater which had a rear-opening door, an innovation at that time. A curved windscreen replaced the original divided one. The extra weight meant that the Vantage engine was fitted as standard but it was soon replaced, from April 1954, by an enlarged, race-proven, 3 litre unit. Top speed rose to 118mph (190km/h).

A Mark II version followed for 1956 which was outwardly similar but identifiable by its more angular rear wings. Although the drophead option continued, there was also a notchback version which lacked the rear door.

The final version, the DB Mark III, was launched at the 1957 Geneva Motor Show. This differed visually by having a new front end with a curved radiator grille and lower bonnet line. It concealed a revised 162bhp engine and the company's competition experience was reflected in the optional fitment of front Girling disc brakes that had been developed on the company's DB3S sports racer. Originally only available for export, American influence was reflected when an automatic gearbox became available for 1959. Production ceased that year as the III made way for the DB4, a total of 1724 examples of the line having been built since 1950.

Above: A DB2/4 with a one-piece windscreen rather than the divided one of its predecessor and two small seats introduced in the rear.

Left: The DB2's interior. The rubber heel pad on the driver's side is an original fitting, as is the grab handle on the passenger's.

Specification	Aston Martin DB Mark III
Engine location	Front, in-line
Configuration	Six-cylinder
Bore and stroke	83 x 90mm
Capacity	2992cc
Valve operation	Twin overhead camshafts
Horsepower	162bhp @ 5500rpm
Transmission	Manual four-speed
Drive	Rear
Chassis	Tubular square section
Suspension – front	Trailing arms and coil spring
Suspension – rear	Radius arm and coil spring
Brakes	Front disc, rear drum
Top speed	118mph (190km/h)
Acceleration	0-60mph (0-96km/h): 9.4 seconds

Below: *This is the prototype Continental of 1951, affectionately known as 'Olga' on account of its distinctive number plate, which happily escaped from the factory. Its roof is 1in (25mm) higher than the production versions.*

Bentley Continental

Top speed 115mph 185km/h

With a top speed of 115mph (185km/h), and clothed in a handsome and distinctive fastback body by H.J. Mulliner, the Bentley Continental of 1952 was, in its day, the fastest production four-seater car in the world.

Destined for a seven-year manufacturing life, the Continental was a spiritual successor of the Bentley Corniche, an experimental aerodynamic saloon of 1939 that did not enter production because of the outbreak of war. As such, it was a model that carried on the traditions of the well-appointed intercontinental grand tourers that were popular in the 1930s.

In 1946 Rolls-Royce introduced its Silver Wraith and related Bentley Mark VI lines. While the former was only available with bespoke coachwork, over 80 per cent of the Bentleys were fitted with a standardized four-door saloon body by Pressed Steel.

Corniche II

Based on the R-Type chassis that was to replace the Mark VI frame in 1952, Rolls-Royce had begun work on what had been internally coded 'Corniche

Right: *The Continental's driving compartment with the polished walnut dashboard almost wholly occupied by instruments. The right-hand gear change is clearly visible.*

II' in 1950. The emphasis was placed firmly on aerodynamic refinement and weight-saving and the memorable body was styled by RR's Ivan Evernden. However, the saloon's 4.6 litre, overhead inlet/side exhaust engine had its compression ratio raised from 6.4 to 7.3:1 and a new exhaust system was fitted.

The prototype, completed in August 1951, was taken to the Montlhéry racing circuit near Paris where it proceeded to average 118.75mph (191.1km/h) over five laps.

Announced in February 1952, the Continental was priced at £6929, which made it one of the most expensive cars on the market. Initially it was only available for export but a right-hand-drive version appeared for the 1953 season.

In the event the overwhelming majority of the 208 R-Type Continentals built were sold in Britain, which accounted for 108 of them. France was in second place with 33, followed by America's 28, and Switzerland's 24. Belgium, Canada and Portugal each took two cars apiece.

Engine capacity increased

After two years in production, in July 1954 the capacity of the Continental's engine was increased to 4.9 litres and four-speed automatic transmission became an option.

In 1955 came the S-Series saloon, the Bentley version of the Rolls-Royce Silver Cloud, both of which used Pressed Steel bodywork. However, the bespoke Continental option was perpetuated although the resulting car was slightly longer than its predecessor because of a new lengthened chassis. The model remained in production until 1959. Its demise spelt the end, for the time being at least, of a Bentley with a purpose-designed body. However, the concept was later revived with the Continental R of 1991.

Specification	Bentley Continental (R-Type)
Engine location	Front, in-line
Configuration	Six-cylinder
Bore and stroke	92 x 114mm
Capacity	4566cc
Valve operation	Overhead inlet/side exhaust
Horsepower	Not disclosed
Transmission	Manual four-speed
Drive	Rear
Chassis	Channel section
Suspension – front	Wishbones and coil spring
Suspension – rear	Half-elliptic spring
Brakes	Drum with mechanical servo
Top speed	115mph (185km/h)
Acceleration	0-60mph (0-96km/h): 13.5 seconds

Above: The view that most other drivers experienced when a Bentley Continental overtook them! To help keep weight down, the bumpers were made of heavy-gauge light alloy. The boot was commodious and the tools and jack were carried in a separate compartment.

Left: Originally the rear wheels were covered with spats in the interests of aerodynamic efficiency. The stop lights mounted on each wing doubled as flashing indicators at a time when semaphore units were the norm. There were also twin reversing lights positioned alongside the number plate.

Chevrolet Corvette

The first of a legendary line, the Corvette was created by America's General Motors Corporation in response to the British open two-seaters that were increasingly appearing, albeit in modest numbers, on American roads during the early 1950s.

The result was distinctly transatlantic in flavour, to European eyes, a garish open two-seater body created by GM's styling supremo, Harley Earl. Because of the low production volumes envisaged, it was made of glass fibre. This was mounted on a bespoke chassis and under the bonnet was a 235cid (3.8 litre) six-cylinder engine: two-speed automatic transmission, with a floor gear change, was fitted.

In truth this first Corvette of 1953 was a bit of a horror but then America's last true sports car had been the Mercer Raceabout of 1911! Only available in that first year in polo white with a red interior, GM's first performance model was marred by indifferent handling, a worrying characteristic when the top speed was an alarming 105mph (169km/h). Against a background of poor sales, the Corporation contemplated scrapping the 'Vette but wisely, in 1955, replaced the six with a 265cid (4.3 litre) V8. A three-speed manual gearbox arrived for

the 1956 season. Performance perked up and the car was now capable of speeds nudging the 120mph (193km/h) mark.

All-new design

The body was rethought for 1956 with the unveiling of an all-new design – the hitherto rather bland profile was enhanced by the introduction of sculptured side panels which were sometimes finished in a contrasting colour. A detachable hardtop was an option and quadruple headlights followed in 1958.

Opposite below: This is one of only a handful or so '55 Corvettes to be six-cylinder-powered. Most used the V8 engine, a configuration which would apply to every 'Vette from then on.

Right: Exterior of the same 1955 car with smoother body panels than previously – teething production bugs of the two previous years had been ironed out.

Right: A 1955 Corvette's dashboard with centrally positioned rev counter. This is one of a few cars built in that model year to be fitted with a manual gearbox.

Top speed
105mph
169km/h

Millionaire racer

The engine's capacity had been upped to 283cid (4.6 litres) for the 1957 season and, interestingly, fuel injection was available as an option although initially it proved to be unreliable. More significantly, in 1960 American millionaire Briggs Cunningham entered a team of three Corvettes in that year's Le Mans race. Although he crashed in the third hour, one car was placed a creditable eighth and the other also finished.

More changes were in store: in 1961 further body refinements included a neatly sculptured tail, which was the work of William Mitchell who had replaced Earl in 1958. Performance was now top of the agenda and in 1962 the engine was again enlarged, this time to 327cid (5.3 litres).

With the Corvette now capable of 150mph (241km/h), Mitchell opted for a complete facelift. The result for the 1963 season was the Sting Ray, arguably the most memorable Corvette of all.

Below: A 1955 Corvette, the first year in which the model was powered by a V8. A 265cid unit was fitted, the CheVrolet script on the side of the front wing being so embellished.

Specification	**Chevrolet** Corvette (1953)
Engine location	Front, in-line
Configuration	Six-cylinder
Bore and stroke	3.56 x 3.93in (90 x 100mm)
Capacity	235cid (3.8 litres)
Valve operation	Pushrod
Horsepower	150bhp @ 4200rpm
Transmission	Automatic two-speed
Drive	Rear
Chassis	Box section
Suspension – front	Wishbones and coil spring
Suspension – rear	Half-elliptic spring
Brakes	Drum
Top speed	105mph (169km/h)
Acceleration	0-60 mph (96km/h): 11.2 seconds

Mercedes-Benz 300SL

One of the truly delectable dream cars, the 300SL coupé is forever remembered for its upward-opening gullwing doors to the extent that its 140mph (225km/h) top speed, fast now but truly sensational in 1954, is often overlooked. It was an instant thoroughbred.

The 300SL, signifying 3 litre super light, was competition bred, its sports-racing predecessor having appeared in 1952. It was powered by a six-cylinder overhead camshaft engine, courtesy of the 300S road car, but this and other production components imposed a weight penalty. The Stuttgart engineers strove to save precious kilograms by the use of a light, strong, but complex tubular space-frame chassis. This demanded that the tubes should be continued as high as possible along the sides of the driving compartment which, in turn, ruled out the use of conventional doors. The answer was the imaginative and ingenious gullwing units that opened vertically and were hinged along the coupé's roof line.

These cars had dominated the 1952 racing season but they were not campaigned in the following year because corporate resources were dedicated to the successful launch and running of the W196 Formula 1 car.

However, in New York, Max Hoffman, a car dealer *par excellence* who specialized in the import of European sports models, convinced Mercedes-

Below: *The gullwing 300SL in all its glory. The distinctive grille on the front wing was intended to permit hot air to escape from the engine compartment.*

Right: *The steering wheel hinged along its centre to allow the driver to get in. Only left-hand-drive cars were built.*

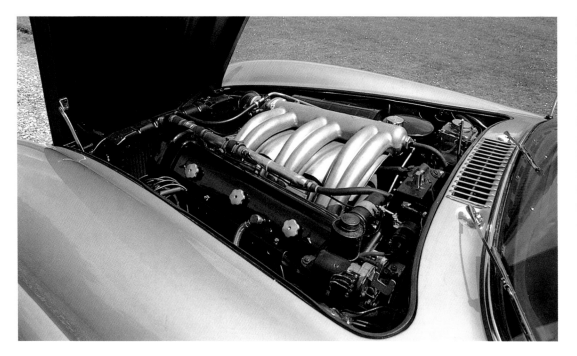

Left: The 300SL's 3 litre, six-cylinder, single-overhead-camshaft engine inclined 50 degrees from the vertical to permit a low bonnet line. Fitted with Bosch fuel injection, it was the first production car to be so equipped. A dry sump unit, it was a modified version of that used in the company's 300 model which appeared in 1951.

Benz of the viability of a roadgoing version of the gorgeous gullwing coupé and promptly ordered 1000. The resulting model was the star of the 1954 New York sports car show.

Racing pedigree

Under the bonnet the 3 litre, six-cylinder, Bosch fuel-injected engine, the first to be fitted in a production car, was inclined to the left to permit a low body line, although this ruled out a right-hand-drive version. The use of dry sump lubrication was a further reminder of the model's racing pedigree while an all-synchromesh gearbox with a floor change, rather than Mercedes' usual column system, was employed.

With room for only two occupants, the steering wheel hinged forward at its lower edge to permit the driver to get in. There was some space behind the seats for luggage but, although the boot outwardly appeared reasonably large, most of the space was occupied by the spare wheel and the large petrol tank.

The coupé's acceleration was phenomenal: it could reach 70mph (113km/h) in second gear and 98mph (158km/h) in third. But handling was tricky and maintenance costs formidable. Nonetheless exactly 1400 examples had been completed when production ceased in 1957. Of these, 29 were lightened cars. These desirable models had all-alloy bodywork and enhanced engines, and were capable of 155mph (249km/h).

Left: One of the famous gullwing doors in the open position. They do take a little time to open and Mercedes-Benz experimented with a variety of handles before finalizing the design. Luggage was stored behind the front seats, the manufacturer offering bespoke suitcases that were held in place with straps to fit into the space.

Specification	Mercedes-Benz 300SL
Engine location	Front, in-line
Configuration	Six-cylinder
Bore and stroke	85 x 88mm
Capacity	2996cc
Valve operation	Single overhead camshaft
Horsepower	190bhp @ 6100rpm
Transmission	Manual four-speed
Drive	Rear
Chassis	Tubular steel space-frame
Suspension – front	Wishbones and coil spring
Suspension – rear	Swing axle and coil spring
Brakes	Drum
Top speed	140mph (225km/h)
Acceleration	0-60mph (0-96km/h): 8.9 seconds

Facel Vega HK500

Launched at the 1954 Paris Salon, the model was the brainchild of Jean Daninos, whose business, *Forges et Ateliers de Construction d'Eure et Loire* (hence Facel), produced specialist car bodies for the likes of Panhard, Simca and Ford France. However, as the mass-produced saloon moved centre stage, this aspect of Daninos' business began to decline, so he decided to produce his own cars. The two-door Facel Vega FVS was the result. The car's appearance was chunky, the twin vertically mounted headlamps distinctive and the well appointed interior was awash with aeronautical themes.

Take a powerful American V8 engine and install it in a distinctive coupé body, complete with aircraft-style controls, and you have the essentials of the Facel Vega, a French make that only survived a mere ten years.

Luxury seating

The instruments extended into a console located between the front seats, establishing a trend in car design that continues to this day. Occupants luxuriously reclined in 'roly-poly' seats.

Refinements included such transatlantic influences as electric windows and the twin radio aerials that sprouted from the rear fins. In fact only one of them was operative!

The engine compartment was pure Detroit. Initially Daninos chose a 4.5 litre 'hemi' Chrysler V8 which had been used in its De Soto make. There was, inevitably, Powerflite two-speed automatic transmission although a manual gearbox was available at extra cost. Even in this form the FVS was capable of some 130mph (209km/h) in the manner of the pre-war *grand routiers* which mopped up the kilometres with such ease.

Top speed
147mph
237km/h

Below: Unmistakable and rapid, the Franco/American Facel Vega HK500 of 1959, by which time right-hand-drive was available. The sills were protected by stainless steel pressings which also made a visual contribution to the design. The deep screen and low bonnet resulted in excellent visibility for the driver.

1960 RV 68

Specification	**Facel Vega** HK500
Engine location	Front, in-line
Configuration	V8
Bore and stroke	104 x 85mm
Capacity	5910cc
Valve operation	Pushrod
Horsepower	360bhp @ 5200rpm
Transmission	Manual four-speed
Drive	Rear
Chassis	Unitary
Suspension – front	Wishbones and coil spring
Suspension – rear	Half-elliptic spring
Brakes	Disc
Top speed	147mph (237km/h)
Acceleration	0-60mph (0-96km/h: 8.5 seconds

Nevertheless, it was not long before Daninos began to opt for larger engines, their capacity first being increased to 4.8, then 5.4 and, ultimately, 5.8 litres. The less popular and unwieldy four-door Excellence followed in 1958.

The HK500, the definitive Facel, appeared in 1959. It was essentially an uprated FVS although it was by then packing a 5.9 litre V8 and 360bhp under its bonnet. Power steering was then well established and the 500 was a 147mph (237km/h) car, even if disc brakes did not arrive until 1960.

The end of the line

The 6.3 litre Facel II, the last of the line, appeared in 1962. It was outwardly more attractive, being lower and more angular, although this was to the detriment of the driving position. There was even more power with a 390bhp option but the model only survived for two years.

Sadly, Daninos' business foundered in 1964, partly because of his decision to introduce the smaller and cheaper Facellia with its own purpose-designed engine.

Above left: The Facel Vega's unusual deeply dished steering wheel. Note the quantity of instrumentation and that the minor controls are located within the innovative central console. The leather-trimmed seats were particularly comfortable, and the cockpit was roomy when judged by the standards of the day.

Left: The twin vertically mounted headlamps dated from the marque's origins in 1954 and were later adopted by the American motor industry in the early 1960s. The steering was moderately low-geared. By this time all-round Dunlop disc brakes had been fitted. In truth, the expensive, well-equipped HK500 had no direct rivals.

Porsche 356 Carrera

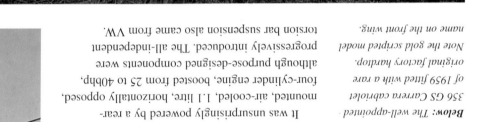

The 356, the first model in the fabled Porsche line, appeared in 1948. The Carrera version, named in celebration of Porsche's successes in the 1952/54 Carrera Panamerica Mexico races, was a potent, noisy, yet highly desirable derivative.

The Stuttgart-based Porsche design bureau was responsible for the creation of the Volkswagen Beetle, destined to be the world's best-selling car. So when Dr Ferdinand's son, Ferry, decided to produce a sports cars, it was inevitably based on VW mechanicals that were cloaked in an aerodynamically refined body produced in mainly coupé and also cabriolet (open) forms.

It was unsurprisingly powered by a rear-mounted, air-cooled, 1.1 litre, horizontally opposed, four-cylinder engine, boosted from 25 to 40bhp, although purpose-designed components were progressively introduced. The all-independent torsion bar suspension also came from VW.

Top-of-the-range

For 1956 Porsche introduced the revised 1.6 litre 356A with the Carrera being the top-of-the-range car. Its 100bhp, 1.5 litre engine (courtesy of the company's 550 Spyder 1955 sports racer) was detuned for road use. Instead of employing the usual pushrods, a train of gears actuated inclined

Top speed
125mph
201km/h

Right: The presence of the legendary Carrera name on the rear engine cover informed other motorists that this was a rather special 356.

Below: The well-appointed 356 GS Carrera cabriolet of 1959 fitted with a rare original factory hardtop. Note the gold scripted model name on the front wing.

Left: The driving compartment of the 1959 GS Carrera with its de luxe leather trim showing to advantage. The gear lever operated a four-speed gearbox, a great virtue of which was that unbeatable synchromesh was fitted to all gears. This was Porsche's own patented baulk ring system.

Below: The 1963 Carrera 2, introduced in the previous year, was the fastest Porsche of its day, even if the company still claimed a top speed of 125mph (201km/h)! The enlarged 2-litre engine developed 130bhp; the model remained in limited production until 1965.

valves in hemispherical cylinder heads. There was a built-up roller bearing Hirth crankshaft with roller conrods and dual ignition which serviced two spark plugs per cylinder.

This raucous power unit endowed the Carrera with a top speed nudging the 125mph (201km/h) mark and made it the fastest 1.5 litre car of its day. Available in coupé, cabriolet, hardtop and no-frills two-seater Speedster forms, the only outwardly visible indication of its power was a gold-finished *Carrera* badge on the engine cover.

From 1958 engine capacity was increased to 1.6 litres. In a bid to quieten the beast, the original crankshaft was replaced by a conventional plain bearing unit.

The mainstream 356B line arrived for 1960 and the Carrera 2 version followed in 1962. This was powered by a 2 litre, 130bhp engine which produced about the same top speed as the original, although acceleration was improved. It also had the virtue of being the first Porsche road car to be fitted with all-round disc brakes.

Extensively raced and rallied, the Carrera was discontinued in 1965 as the company's purpose-designed sports racers moved centre stage. However, the name has remained as an intrinsic and respected part of the Porsche model range ever since.

Specification	Porsche Carrera (1.5 litre)
Engine location	Rear, in-line
Configuration	Horizontally opposed four-cylinder
Bore and stroke	85 x 66mm
Capacity	1498cc
Valve operation	Twin overhead camshafts per bank
Horsepower	115bhp @ 6200rpm
Transmission	Manual four-speed
Drive	Rear
Chassis	Platform
Suspension – front	Trailing arms and torsion bar
Suspension – rear	Swing axle and torsion bar
Brakes	Drum
Top speed	125mph (201km/h)
Acceleration	0-60mph (0-96km/h): 11.3 seconds

Austin-Healey 3000

Top speed
114mph
183km/h

The rugged Big Healey of the 1960s, with no-nonsense specifications and a consistent rallying record, owed its origins to the Healey 100 of 1952 which was the brainchild of successful pre-war rally driver Donald Healey. He had initially produced, in Warwick between 1946 and 1952, a range of Riley-engined models that were costly, heavy but potent.

The single-minded Cornishman soon realized that he ought to create a smaller, cheaper, open sports car of a type that was introducing America to the delights of two-seater motoring. The 1.8 litre Austin-engined Healey 100 accordingly made its debut at the 1952 London Motor Show. It was immediately commandeered by Leonard Lord, chairman of the newly formed British Motor Corporation that was a merger of the Austin and Morris motor businesses.

Overnight Donald's roadster became the Austin-Healey 100, so styled to reflect the fact that it was capable of 100mph (161km/h) and was BMC's corporate sports car. It was produced in this form until 1956 when the four-cylinder engine was replaced by a 2.6 litre six. Renamed the 100/6 and available in two- and more popular two-plus-two seater guises, it was, if anything, slower than the model it replaced! Fortunately this shortcoming was rectified by the adoption, from the 1958 season, of a six-port cylinder head.

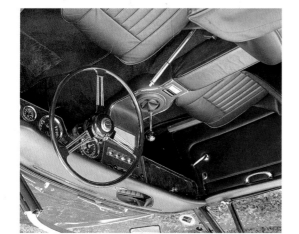

In 1957 production was transferred from Austin's Longbridge factory to MG's Abingdon works and two years later the engine's capacity was increased to 3 litres. Arriving for 1960, the appropriately renamed 3000 greatly benefited from the bigger-bored 132bhp engine. It was capable, in overdrive top, of speeds approaching the 115mph (185km/h) mark. This speed required the fitment of front disc brakes.

Although raced and rallied by BMC on both sides of the Atlantic, in the event these rugged, reliable but pushrod-engined cars were invariably outpaced by the consistently faster 3 litre Ferraris with overhead camshafts.

Right: A Mark III 3000 produced for the 1964 model year – this was a more civilized offering with a revised dashboard with wood veneer central console complete with cubby box, and wind-up windows. The seats were also improved, including the smaller occasional rear ones.

Below right: A Mark II car with factory hardtop and the sliding side screens in place. This example has non-standard vents cut into the front wings to permit hot air to escape from the engine compartment. The wire wheels were also a desirable optional extra, but usually discs ones were fitted as standard.

Opposite: A Mark II car of 1961. Produced between 1961 and 1963, it is instantly identifiable by the radiator grille's vertical bars; its Mark I predecessor's were horizontal. There is also a small MK II badge placed beneath the winged Austin-Healey motif.

The last of the line

The Mark II 3000 of 1961 was briefly offered with triple carburettors although it reverted to twins in 1962. The last of the line, the Mark III of 1963, was only produced in two-plus-two form – by then the engine was boosted to 150bhp.

The Big Healey died in 1968, following the absorption of BMC by the Leyland Corporation. The new owner was reluctant to continue paying royalties to an outside contractor who built what had become an outdated design.

Although Donald Healey attempted to fill the gap left in America by the 3000's demise with the smaller Jensen-Healey of 1972/76, it proved to be a pale shadow of the original.

Specification	Austin-Healey 3000 Mark I
Engine location	Front, in-line
Configuration	Six-cylinder
Bore and stroke	83 x 88mm
Capacity	2912cc
Valve operation	Pushrod
Horsepower	124bhp @ 4600rpm
Transmission	Manual four-speed with overdrive
Drive	Rear
Chassis	Platform
Suspension – front	Wishbones and coil spring
Suspension – rear	Half-elliptic spring
Brakes	Front disc, rear drum
Top speed	114mph (183km/h)
Acceleration	0-60mph (0-96km/h): 11.5 seconds

Jaguar E-Type

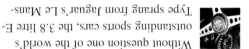

Top speed
150mph
241km/h

Without question one of the world's outstanding sports cars, the 3.8 litre E-Type sprang from Jaguar's Le Mans-winning D-Type and caused a sensation on its announcement at the 1961 Geneva Motor Show. Appearing first in hardtop coupé form with a useful rear opening door, a roadster soon followed. Certainly the E-Type's looks were sufficient to ensure immortality. Jaguar claimed a top speed of 150mph (241km/h) but, in truth, only a few carefully assembled examples were capable of this figure. The £2000 price tag ensured that the model was destined for a long production run, and in fact it survived in this form until 1971.

Independent rear suspension, created for the impending Mark X saloon, featured for the first time on a Jaguar sports car, while all-round disc brakes, honed on the motor racing circuits, were fitted front and rear.

Below: *The Series III E-Type, introduced in 1971, was the first recipient of Jaguar's long-awaited 5.3 litre V12 engine. Identifiable by its enlarged radiator grille and flared wheel arches, this example has been fitted with optional wire wheels. It was similarly produced in coupé form.*

Triumph of styling

Stylistically the E-Type's lines were a triumph for Jaguar's aerodynamicist Malcolm Sayer, who also had the bodies of the sports racing C and D-Types to his credit. For once Jaguar's chairman, William Lyons, who usually styled the company's products, took a back seat.

Like the E-Type's XK120 predecessor, the new model found immediate favour in America where it was known as the XK-E, and no less than 80 per cent of production was exported there.

For 1966 the E-Type was fitted with a 4.2 litre engine which did not push the top speed but improved bottom end torque. An all-synchromesh gearbox replaced the unrefined Moss unit which lacked synchromesh on the bottom cog.

The original version was strictly a two-seater but 1966 saw the arrival of a 2+2 E-Type coupé which offered rear seating for two small children.

This extended the model's appeal. On the debit side, the redesign caused a dilution of those impeccable lines and increased weight.

The American market

A Series II E-Type arrived for 1969. It was revised to take account of American safety and emissions regulations. It was outwardly identifiable by its forward-mounted open headlamps, which dispensed with the previous perspex covers, and an enlarged radiator intake. The interior was also revised with tumbler switches replacing the more attractive but projecting lever-type units. But under the bonnet detoxing the engine for the US market meant 171 rather than 265bhp and a top speed of 'only' 125mph (201km/h).

The Series II was discontinued in 1971, when the Series III version appeared on the 2+2 chassis powered by Jaguar's long-awaited 5.3 litre V12 engine. Less of sports car, more of a grand tourer, it survived until 1975. By then the twin effects of soaring petrol prices and advancing age spelt the end of what had become a motoring legend in its own lifetime.

Below: The superlative lines of a 1962 E-Type coupé are shown to good effect. Unusually, this particular example raced at Le Mans.

Bottom left: The 'office' of a 4.2 litre E-Type with the original flick switches that survived until 1969.

Specification	**Jaguar** E-Type (3.8 litres)
Engine location	Front, in-line
Configuration	Six-cylinder
Bore and stroke	87 x 106mm
Capacity	3781cc
Valve operation	Twin overhead camshafts
Horsepower	265bhp @ 5500rpm
Transmission	Manual four-speed
Drive	Rear
Chassis	Monocoque/squared tubular front sub-frame
Suspension – front	Wishbones and torsion bar
Suspension – rear	Wishbone and coil spring
Brakes	Disc
Top speed	150mph (241km/h) but see text
Acceleration	0-60mph (0-96km/h): 7 seconds

AC Cobra

Top speed 138mph 222km/h

One hundred miles an hour (161km/h) coming up in 14 seconds is still a very respectable acceleration figure today – in the 1960s it was truly sensational. The AC Cobra, in which a lusty American V8 engine replaced a British power unit of a mere 2 litres capacity, was one of the truly great performance cars of the post-war years.

The Cobra was rooted in AC's Ace of 1954, an open two-seater sports cars with a tubular chassis and all-independent transverse leaf suspension. This behaved best when powered by a 2 litre Bristol engine, which was an alternative to the Thames Ditton's company's own 2 litre six, although the last of the line used a 2.5 litre Ford Zephyr unit.

Then American racing driver Carroll Shelby approached AC with a view to extending the Ace's

Below: An AC 289 of 1966, this example has been in the same ownership since new. Produced for the European market, this was AC's version of the Cobra, but under a different name. The lines of the Ace, on which it was based, are readily apparent in the styling.

life with a 260cid (4.2 litre) V8, courtesy of Ford of America. He proposed that left-hand-drive cars should be built without engines at AC's factory and then shipped to California where he would install their power units. The resulting car would be called the AC Shelby-Cobra, the name having come to him in a dream!

AC Shelby-Cobra in production

The British company agreed to this proposal and the car was announced in the autumn of 1962. After the first 75 had been completed, the original engine was replaced by a 289cid (4.7 litre) unit. Performance of this Mark II was excellent for its day, top speed being 138mph (222km/h).

But the engine transplant displayed the limitations of the 1954 vintage suspension and Shelby initiated, with Ford input, the uprated Mark

Left: All beef and muscle: a 427 Mark III Cobra, shod with the appropriate Halibrand alloy wheels. Left-hand-drive, of course.

Below left: The Mark III engine with the Shelby-fitted rocker covers which replaced the original pressed steel ones.

Below: UK Cobra guru Rod Leach at the wheel of the impressivly powerful 427. The front wing vent permits hot air to escape from the engine compartment.

III Cobra of 1965 with a wider chassis and all-round wishbones and coil spring suspension. A 427cid (6.9 litre) V8 was now employed and the Halibrand alloy wheels required even wider wheel arches. In this form what was now called the Shelby-Cobra was capable of 165mph (265km/h). It continued to be sold until 1968.

Right-hand-drive Cobras had been available on the British market since 1964. The Mark III, though fitted with the 4.7 litre V8, was marketed as the AC 289 in Britain between 1966 and 1968 because AC did not own the rights to the Cobra name.

After a hiatus, in 1983 the Cobra concept was revived in Britain. Initially the 4.9 litre AC Mark IV could not be called a Cobra but in 1986 permission for use of the name was forthcoming from Ford, which by then owned it. The car remains in limited production at the time of writing (2001), no less than 40 years since this ingenious Anglo-American sports car was first conceived.

Specification	**AC** Shelby-Cobra Mark II
Engine location	Front, in-line
Configuration	V8
Bore and stroke	4.0 x 2.87in (101 x 72mm)
Capacity	289cid (4735cc)
Valve operation	Pushrod
Horsepower	300bhp @ 5700rpm
Transmission	Manual four-speed
Drive	Rear
Chassis	Tubular steel
Suspension – front	Transverse leaf spring and wishbones
Suspension – rear	Transverse leaf spring and wishbones
Brakes	Disc
Top speed	138mph (222km/h)
Acceleration	0-60mph (0-96km/h): 5.6 seconds

Right: *The Zagato's lines shown to advantage. The transparent headlamp covers were fitted in the interests of aerodynamic efficiency. All the cars differ slightly in details and, of the 19 cars built, all survive. The only 'missing' car was discovered in Italy in 1974.*

Above: *A 1962 right-hand-drive Zagato, arguably the best and most original of the cars as it was purchased new in October of that year by J.E. Beck of Cheshire, who kept it for many years. Note the absence of a rear bumper.*

Aston Martin DB4 GT Zagato

Top speed 152mph 244km/h

In October 1958 Aston Martin unveiled its acclaimed Touring-styled DB4 and a lighter, shortened, faster GT version followed a year later. Then, at the 1960 London Motor Show, the memorable and even more potent DB4 GT Zagato appeared. It was so named because it was bodied in Italy by the Zagato styling house of Milan.

Visually stunning

The work of the talented young Ercole Spada, 'the Zagato', as it was invariably known, was a visually stunning competition car although it was also available in roadgoing form.

Under the bonnet was a high specification version of the DB4's twin-overhead-camshaft 3.6 litre engine. Originally developing 240bhp, the GT version was boosted to a claimed 302bhp, actually 267, thanks to 9:1 rather than 8.2 compression ratio, special high lift camshafts, twin sparking plugs per cylinder and triple Weber carburettors in place of the original twin SUs. Running on a 9.7:1 compression, the Zagatos' engines were further boosted to 285bhp.

At 2800lb (1270kg), the tubular-framed, purposeful, alloy coupés were about 100lb (45kg) lighter than the factory GTs and could attain over 150mph (241km/h). Once completed, the cars were returned to Aston Martin's Newport Pagnell works for trimming, although a few examples were completed by Zagato.

Like the factory DB4 GTs, there were only two seats in the front. The space usually occupied by the rear seat was occupied by a platform for the storage of luggage.

Over the next three years a total of 19 cars was completed, each one differing slightly from the others. Production was almost evenly split with ten right-hand-drive examples built while the remainder were left hookers. Perversely, one chassis was bodied by Bertone.

Essex Racing Stables

Aston Martin had withdrawn from sports-car racing in 1959 so the Zagatos were campaigned on the racing circuits during 1961 and 1962 by privateers, most significantly John Ogier's Essex Racing Stables which ran two of them memorably registered 1 VEV and 2 VEV. While the cars invariably finished in GT races in Britain and on the Continent, they were unable to hold their own against the might of Ferrari's GTOs.

Although production ceased in 1963, this was not quite the end of the story. In 1991 Aston Martin decided to utilize four unused chassis numbers that had been allocated to the original series. Zagato

Specification	**Aston Martin** DB4 GT Zagato
Engine location	Front, in-line
Configuration	Six-cylinder
Bore and stroke	92 x 92mm
Capacity	3670cc
Valve operation	Twin overhead camshafts
Horsepower	285bhp @ 6000rpm
Transmission	Manual four-speed
Drive	Rear
Chassis	Platform
Suspension – front	Wishbones and coil spring
Suspension – rear	Trailing link, Watt's linkage/coil spring
Brakes	Disc
Top speed	152mph (244km/h)
Acceleration	0-60mph (0-96km/h:) 6.2 seconds

produced a further four cars under the Sanction II designation, outwardly almost identical to the originals and with only detail differences to their specifications. Otherwise they remained true to the 1960 classic design.

Top left: Cockpit of a left-hand-drive Zagato. The seven instruments can be clearly seen through the wood-rimmed steering wheel. The seats, which are adjustable for rake, are supportive while the pedals are well positioned.

Top right: The Zagato's engine with the DB4 GT's twin-plug cylinder head serviced by distributors driven off the bulkhead end of each camshaft. The triple Weber carburettors on the far side of the engine use a cool air intake box.

Left: Strictly a two-seater, the Zagato still looks good some 50 years after its first appearance. Made of light alloy, it is vulnerable to damage. Note the Z monogram ahead of the air intake on the front wing, so there can be no doubt of the body's origins!

Ferrari 250 GTO

One of the rarest (just 39 were built) and today the most collectible and expensive of Ferraris, the legendary GTO was created for the newly introduced GT World Championship of 1962. A sports racer that could also be used as a road car, it was capable of a blistering 185mph (298km/h).

The car was engineered by Giotto Bizzarrini, who was later to be responsible for Lamborghini's enduring V12 engine. Unusually he not only laid out the chassis but also the sensational lines of the Ferrari's berlinetta body, a task usually undertaken by Pininfarina.

The resulting design was not only supremely elegant but utterly distinctive, for Bizzarrini also recognized the importance of improving a car's performance by aerodynamic refinement and he accordingly undertook airflow experiments in Pisa University's wind tunnel. The results were confirmed during testing at the Modena and Monza circuits and even on the Italian autostradas, no doubt to the delight of other motorists.

Distinctive rear spoiler

The Scaglietti-built body's distinctive rear spoiler helped to kept the wheels of the 295bhp 3 litre V12 on the road. This proven and reliable power unit was inherited from the GTO's open sports-racing Testa Rossa predecessor.

The car was the ultimate development of Ferrari's 250 GT of 1955, which was produced in short wheelbase form for the racetrack from 1959.

Right: *The GTO's engine with the 12 stacks of inlet ports for the six Weber carburettors was apparent. With weight an ever-present consideration, the cam covers were made of magnesium.*

Below: *The semi-circular air intakes could be covered and were opened to increase air flow to the engine at slow speeds. The apertures below the headlamps direct air to the brakes.*

Top speed
185mph
298km/h

The GTO title stood for *Gran Turismo Omologato* – in other words homologated, a racing stipulation which required that 100 examples of a particular car be constructed. After some controversy with the authorities, Enzo Ferrari got around the problem by proclaiming that he had been producing 3 litre GTs since 1955!

Although the overwhelming majority of GTOs were 3 litre powered, there was a trio of 4 litre models. It was typical of Ferrrari that while much attention was lavished on the engine and body, the tubular chassis featured conventional wishbones and coil springs and the essentials of a cart-sprung rear which had not been much updated since 1947.

Created for the new 3 litre GT World Championship, the GTO not only gave Ferrari victory in 1962 but also in 1963 and 1964. The latter year proved to be the last for this potent and, it should be said, beautiful and purposeful car.

Success on the racing circuits

The GTO had proved itself invincible on the GT racing circuits and an example was placed second at Le Mans in 1962. It was only displaced in the mid-1960s when rear-engined sports racers, following in the wheeltracks of Formula 1 cars, gained the upper hand.

In 1965 the Maranello company decided to concentrate all its efforts on Formula 1 and prototype sports car racing. Ferrari therefore bowed out from GT competition after a highly successful decade, mostly spent on top.

Above: The GTO looks just as good from the rear. The large air outlet positioned on the rear wing allowed hot air generated by the back tyres and brakes to escape more quickly.

Below left: The instrument panel was dominated by a revolution counter; all the dials can be easily seen through the spokes of the lovely Nardi aluminium and wood steering wheel.

Specification	Ferrari GTO
Engine location	Front, in-line
Configuration	V12
Bore and stroke	73 x 58mm
Capacity	2953cc
Valve operation	Twin overhead camshafts per bank
Horsepower	295bhp @ 7400rpm
Transmission	Manual five-speed
Drive	Rear
Chassis	Tubular steel
Suspension – front	Wishbones and coil spring
Suspension – rear	Half-elliptic springs, radius arms and Watts linkage
Brakes	Disc
Top speed	185mph (298km/h)
Acceleration	N/A

Chevrolet Sting Ray

Below: *Well proportioned and distinctive, a 1963 Corvette roadster. The dummy hot air outlets were opened up in 1965 to duct heat away from the engine.*

The Corvette Sting Ray with its glass-fibre body, finely chiselled lines and concealed headlights came of age in the 1963 season. For, apart from its V8 engine, there were no legacies from earlier 'Vettes, and the car was based on a new all-independent suspension chassis to the benefit of roadholding.

Its memorable and distinctive aerodynamically-honed styling was the work of William Mitchell, General Motors' head of styling, who was much more susceptible to European influences than his predecessor Harley Earl. And while the Sting Ray possessed its own distinctive personality, the stylistic subtleties of Jaguar's superlative E-Type were readily apparent (Mitchell was an enthusiastic owner/driver of one).

Further visual input came from two of Mitchell's experimental cars, the 1958 Stingray two-seater racer and XP-720 coupé of 1959. The latter was significant because the '63 Corvette was

Top speed 142mph 228km/h

Right: The 'Ray's engine was a 327cid V8, introduced in 1962. Developing 250bhp, a more powerful 365bhp unit was available at extra cost.

to be offered in coupé form in the Continental European manner and the style has been an enduring feature of the line ever since.

'Father of the Corvette', Belgian-born engineer Zora Arkus-Duntov, was intent that the Sting Ray would offer better interior accommodation than its predecessor, along with better handling. This was

achieved, despite the fact that the car had a shorter wheelbase, at 98in (2489 mm), than the 1953-62 generation's 102in (2590mm). To allow for this, there was a new box-section chassis and rear transverse leaf spring/radius rod independent suspension demanded by the body's design.

Speed in excess of 140mph

The engine was the previous year's 327cid (5.3 litre) V8 which was to be available in 250 and 365hp guises during the Sting Ray's production life. The latter powered the model to over 140mph (225km/h). Fuel injection, introduced in 1957, remained as an option until 1966.

There were further engine enhancements in the pipeline and in 1965 a 396cid (6.5 litre) V8 appeared. This was the year in which the Corvette was also provided with all-round disc brakes. Yet a further engine option arrived for 1966, in the form of a 427cid (7 litre) V8; however, less desirably, the model's increased weight dropped its top speed to 135mph (217km/h).

Outwardly the classic lines remained essentially unchanged during the 'Ray's six-year production life, although the coupé underwent a small but significant modification from the 1964 season. Mitchell had initially insisted on a divided rear window but this was deleted on the grounds that it restricted visibility. But he has had the last word because today collectors are queuing up to buy pre-1964 examples…

The line was discontinued in 1967 after some 180,000 Sting Rays had been completed. A legend was in the making.

Above: The Corvette acquired a coupé body with the Sting Ray. This 1963 car is identifiable by its now highly desirable divided rear window which was deleted in 1964. The fact that the doors intrude into the roof is a nice touch.

Specification	**Chevrolet** Corvette Sting Ray (327cid)
Engine location	Front, in-line
Configuration	V8
Bore and stroke	4.0 x 3.25in (101 x 82mm)
Capacity	327cid (5358cc)
Valve operation	Pushrod
Horsepower	250bhp @ 4400rpm
Transmission	Manual three-speed
Drive	Rear
Chassis	Perimeter
Suspension – front	Wishbones and transverse leaf spring
Suspension – rear	Radius rod and transverse leaf spring
Brakes	Drum
Top speed	142mph (228km/h)
Acceleration	0-60mph (0-96km/h): 5.9 seconds

Pontiac GTO

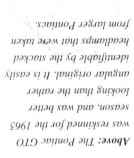

The GTO was the car that ushered in America's muscle car era. Destined to revitalize Pontiac's sales in the booming youth market of the 1960s, such was the success of this outwardly deceptive model that the rest of the American motor industry wasted little time in following suit.

It was in January 1963 that Pontiac advertising executive Jim Wagners (or engineers John DeLorean and Bill Collins depending on who was telling the story) decided to insert a 389cid (6.4 litre) V8 under the bonnet of Pontiac's newly minted Tempest line.

Development undertaken in secret

The only trouble was that Pontiac was a division of General Motors and there was a corporate ban on engines larger than 330cid (5.4 litres) powering an intermediate model such as the two-door Tempest. Development work was consequently undertaken in secrecy with prototypes fitted with '326' V8s although, in reality, they carried the larger capacity 389 unit.

Pontiac got around the corporate diktat by making what it named the GTO. The appellation was filched from the Ferrari of the same name, the initials standing for *Gran Turismo Omologato*, an option in the Tempest Le Mans series.

The model, introduced for 1964, was available in sports coupé, hardtop and convertible forms. It used the 389 unit with distinctive chromed valve covers, enhanced by a 'hotter' camshaft and High Output cylinder heads which were crowned by a Carter four barrel carburettor. Available in two states of tune, the standard was 325hp and there was an optional 348 version.

Selling for a highly competitive $3400, the GTO could reach 60mph (96km/h) in around 4.5 seconds and top speed was in excess of 110mph (177km/h). Such performance had not previously been available at this price.

The following year's GTO underwent a reskin and was easily identifiable by its vertically

Above: The Pontiac GTO was reskinned for the 1965 season, and was better looking than the rather angular original. It is easily identifiable by the stacked headlamps that were taken from larger Pontiacs.

Right: The GTO name lingered on until 1974, its performance image being a victim of the depression fuelled by the oil price rise. This is the GTO 400 version of the two-door Pontiac Le Mans. Note its curious bonnet scoops.

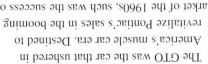

Specification	**Pontiac** GTO
Engine location	Front, in-line
Configuration	V8
Bore and stroke	4.06 x 3.75in (103 x 95mm)
Capacity	389cid (6374cc)
Valve operation	Pushrod
Horsepower	325bhp @ 4800rpm
Transmission	Manual three-speed
Drive	Rear
Chassis	Box section
Suspension – front	Wishbones and coil spring
Suspension – rear	Trailing links and coil spring
Brakes	Drum
Top speed	110mph (177km/h)
Acceleration	0-60mph (0-96km/h): 6.9 seconds

Above left: An optional bonnet-mounted revolution counter appeared on the GTO 400 during the 1967 model year.

Left: The GTO convertible for the 1967 season was essentially the same as the previous year's cars, apart from more visible rear lights.

Below: The impressive cockpit with bucket seats, floor gear change and GTO initials proudly emblazoned on the dash.

mounted twin headlamps which replaced the horizontal ones. Otherwise the mechanicals remained the same although the 389's outputs were modestly increased to 335 and 360hp.

There was an impressive and distinctive new GTO for 1966 and demand was such that Pontiac built no less than 96,946 of them in a single year which was a production record for any muscle car. Similarly powered by a 389 engine, this was a 120mph (193km/h) model. The second generation GTO was uprated for the 1967 season with the V8 enlarged to 400cid (6.5 litres). Top speed was now 125mph (201km/h).

The last of the line, the GTO of the 1968-72 era, retained the 400 V8 but also offered an optional 455cid (7.4 litre) unit. But by then Pontiac was concentrating resources on its increasingly potent and popular Firebird line.

Ford GT40

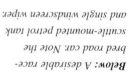

**Top speed
160mph
257km/h**

Below: *A desirable race-
bred road car. Note the
scuttle-mounted petrol tank
and single windscreen wiper.*

Right: *The Mark III's mid-
located Ford V8 engine, this
example exhibiting Cobra-
related Shelby origins.*

Using this ingenious concept as a starting point,
Ford proceeded to develop the design at Slough,
Berkshire in a facility managed by John Wyer,
formerly of Aston Martin. The trio of cars that

Created by Ford with the express aim of
winning the Le Mans 24 hour race, the
Anglo/American GT40 did precisely that
and took the chequered flag there in four successive
years from 1966 to 1969.

However, Ford's Le Mans triumphs were not
lightly won and it took no less than three years to
develop a winning car. Ford was a company used to
producing value-for-money, mass-produced
saloons, and it lacked any experience of creating
such a racer. So it acquired the rights to the
innovative Lola GT, which had run, albeit
unsuccessfully, at the 1963 Le Mans race. Radically
its 4.2 litre Ford V8 engine was mounted
longitudinally behind the driver in the manner of
contemporary Formula 1 cars.

appeared at the 1964 Le Mans event were thus closely related to the Lola, although they were powered by an alloy version of Ford's V8. The GT40 name was adopted because on the road the coupés stood a mere 40in (1016mm) high.

Although spectacularly fast, one was timed at 187mph (301km/h), all the cars suffered from teething troubles, after which Ford transferred the GT40's development to America and placed the project under the control of Carroll Shelby, creator of the AC Cobra.

The original V8 was replaced by a 7 litre unit. Six examples of what was designated the Mark II were run at the 1965 Le Mans event but all succumbed to mechanical failures.

Radical modifications

Further radical modifications followed and in 1966 Ford was triumphant and took the first three places in the 24 hour classic. The following year the Mark IV, with a lighter stronger chassis made of an aluminium honeycomb sandwich material, was also victorious. At this point Ford decided to quit while it was ahead. However, GT40s prepared by John Wyer took the chequered flag at Le Mans for the next two years under the sponsorship of Gulf Oil.

In the meantime Wyer had produced a roadgoing version of the Mark III powered by a 4.7 litre V8. Introduced in December 1965, it cost £6647 and closely resembled the sports racer, apart from a reprofiled nose, twin headlamps which

replaced the single units, and a taller tail that incorporated overheated luggage compartments located either side of the gearbox. Even this tamed version could attain 160mph (257km/h).

Production ceased in 1968, by which time just 31 examples of these fabulous street machines had been completed.

Specification	**Ford** GT40 Mark III (4.7 litres)
Engine location	Mid, in-line
Configuration	V8
Bore and stroke	101 x 72mm
Capacity	4736cc
Valve operation	Pushrod
Horsepower	306bhp @ 6000rpm
Transmission	Manual four-speed
Drive	Rear
Chassis	Steel semi-monocoque
Suspension – front	Wishbone and coil spring
Suspension – rear	Trailing arm, wishbones and coil spring
Brakes	Disc
Top speed	160mph (257km/h)
Acceleration	0-60mph (0-96km/h): 5.3 seconds

Iso Grifo

Top speed
171mph
275Km/h

Seizing on the concept of a potent American V8 shoe-horned into a stylish coupé body, in 1963 the Italian Iso concern produced the Grifo which was one of the fastest GTs of its day and could attain speeds in excess of 180mph (290km/h).

Milan-based motorcycle manufacturer Iso was the creator of the Isetta bubble car: in 1955 it sold the design to BMW and there was to be a seven-year hiatus before it produced another vehicle. In 1960 founder Renzo Rivolta attended the London Motor Show and he was influenced there by the Bertone-styled, Corvette-V8 engined Gordon-Keeble. The result was the 1962 Rivolta GT with body lines similarly essayed by Bertone and powered by a 5.4 litre 300bhp Chevrolet V8. Its chassis was engineered by Giotto Bizzarrini, formerly of Alfa Romeo and Ferrari, and the transmission was of transatlantic origin, being Borg Warner or, later, Powerglide automatics. A five-speed ZF manual gearbox was also available. This paved the way the following year for the lighter and faster two-seater Grifo which used a shortened version of the Rivolta's chassis. It was,

once again, Bertone-bodied although it was far more stylish than its rather soberly styled predecessor. In addition to the mainstream coupé, it was also available with a sun roof, a Targa-type top and as a full roadster.

7 litre version introduced

This initially used the Chevy V8: the 365bhp version was capable of 158mph (254km/h). However, it was also successively available in 350,

Right: *The heart of the Grifo, an American V8 which provided plenty of performance at a reasonable price. This is a 7 litre Chevrolet Corvette unit, but this was later replaced by a smaller capacity Ford one.*

Below: *The fine lines of the Grifo's Bertone body helped to sell a model that was one of the fastest cars in the world. The hot air vents helped keep the engine and rear brakes cool.*

300 and 340hp states of tune. A top-line muscular 7 litre version followed in 1969 which used the Corvette 427 engine, and a 7.4 litre unit followed in 1970. The latter version was fitted with modified bodywork, developed no less than 460bhp and could attain 186mph (299km/h) flat out. Later, in 1973 and 1974, 'smaller' 5.7 litre Ford V8s replaced the Chevvy units.

There was also a sports-racing Grifo A3/C which Bizzarrini produced at his own plant at Livorno. When Iso ceased its racing activities at the end of 1965, he continued to produce the car, which was variously named the Bizzarrini GT Strada or GT America, until 1969.

The Grifo proper ceased production in 1974, by which time 412 examples had been completed. But in 1998 Pietro Rivolta, the founder's son, announced plans for a new Grifo with Zagato-styled composite body and a Ford 4.5 litre V8. Sadly this latter-day car has failed to materialize.

Above: Looking as good from the rear, the twin exhaust pipes reveal the presence of V8 power...

Below left: The Grifo's left-hand-drive interior was very light, thanks to the large rear window.

Specification	**Iso** Grifo (7 litres)
Engine location	Front, in-line
Configuration	V8
Bore and stroke	108 x 95mm
Capacity	6998cc
Valve operation	Pushrod
Horsepower	390bhp @ 5200rpm
Transmission	Manual four-speed
Drive	Rear
Chassis	Unitary
Suspension – front	Wishbones and coil spring
Suspension – rear	De Dion axle, radius arm and coil spring
Brakes	Disc
Top speed	171mph (275km/h)
Acceleration	0-60mph (0-96km/h): 7.1 seconds

Shelby Mustang GT-350

**Top speed
119mph**
191km/h

The sporty Mustang of 1964, the fastest-selling model in Ford's post-war history, spawned a rare and successful track-ready derivative in 1965 in the form of the GT-350.

Commissioned by the company and prepared by Carroll Shelby, creator of the AC Cobra, it was built to challenge the rival Chevrolet Corvette in Sports Car Club of America events and simultaneously to hone Ford's performance image.

Power was boosted to 306bhp

Taking the 2 + 2 GT Mustang coupé as his starting point, Shelby retained the 271bhp 289cid (4.7 litre) V8 but power was boosted to 306bhp by the fitment of a bespoke Holley carburettor, a high rise aluminium inlet manifold and new exhaust system. A Borg-Warner aluminium four-speed close-ratio manual gearbox was employed.

Suspension was uprated and adjustable Koni shock absorbers added. Perversely, the unassisted steering box was removed and replaced by a higher geared powered unit. Inside the trim was discarded and replaced by two competition front seats with the spare tyre taking the place of the rear squab.

As for the name of the conversion, legend has it that this was born during a meeting held at Shelby American's modest factory at Venice, California. When he asked about the distance to a nearby engineering shop, a colleague paced out the gap and declared it to be some 350 feet. So the GT-350 was born…

Shorn of its corporate badges, the Shelby Mustang was unveiled in January 1965 and was offered in two guises. There was a potent 360bhp GT-350R which was intended for racing, but the overwhelming majority of cars were the more tractable GT-350S street machine.

Above: A 1965 Shelby Mustang in obligatory white. The interior is black. Based on the fastback model, the cars were delivered from Ford minus bonnet, exhaust system and back seat, the conversion work being undertaken at Shelby's factory in Venice, California.

Right: The 1965 GT-350 bore a closer resemblance to the production Mustang than 1966 cars. They had plastic rear quarter windows and scoops behind the doors to cool the rear brakes. In both cases the Ford badges were removed.

There was just one exterior finish specified, white, which is America's racing colour, with blue striping that ran along the cars' sills and proclaimed the *GT-350* designation. There were also extra matching 'Le Mans' stripes added to a car's centre-line. Other identifying features were side air scoops introduced ahead of the rear wheel arches while small triangular rear side windows replaced the original louvres.

Racing success

Some 680,000 standard Mustangs were built in 1965 and Shelby's production accounted for a mere 562 examples, of which perhaps 30 were racers. But they did everything expected of them and won that year's SSCA's B-Production National Championship and repeated the success over the next two years.

1966's cars were rather tamer than the originals and the colour range was expanded to embrace red, blue, green and black which were complemented

Specification	Shelby Mustang GT-350
Engine location	Front, in-line
Configuration	V8
Bore and stroke	4.0 x 2.87in (101 x 73mm)
Capacity	289cid (4735cc)
Valve operation	Pushrod
Horsepower	306bhp @ 6000rpm
Transmission	Manual four-speed
Drive	Rear
Chassis	Unitary
Suspension – front	Wishbones and coil spring
Suspension – rear	Half-elliptic springs
Brakes	Front disc, rear drum
Top speed	119mph (191km/h)
Acceleration	0-60mph (0-96km/h): 6.5 seconds

by black or gold racing stripes. Just 2380 were built in 1966 and this included 936 which were rented that year to lucky customers by Hertz. They were invariably returned with telltale signs of racing activity in evidence!

Below: A distinctive plain grille with the famous Mustang motif moved from its customary central position to the side.

Lamborghini Miura

Top speed
171mph
274km/h

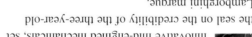

In 1966 the Miura supercar, in which a sensational body was united with innovative mid-engined mechanicals, set the seal on the credibility of the three-year-old Lamborghini marque.

It was the only make to challenge Ferrari's pre-eminent position as Italy's foremost supercar builder. Tractor manufacturer Ferruccio Lamborghini's first model, the 350GT for 1963, was powered by a magnificent 3.5 litre quad-cam V12 engine, designed by former Ferrari engineer Giotto Bizzarrini. Yet although the Touring-designed body was elegant, it lacked that special elusive quality that Lamborghini was seeking.

It arrived in abundance with the Miura. Daringly, Lamborghini's young chief engineer Giampaolo Dallara transferred the 350bhp V12, by then extended to 3.9 litres, from the front of the car to the middle of it. But rather than positioning it longitudinally, Ford GT40-style, he adventurously opted for a transverse configuration in the manner of the British Mini. The five-speed gearbox was similarly located in the engine's sump.

Below: Often hailed as the world's first supercar, the Miura's Bertone body was as stunning as its mid-engined mechanicals that were inspired by Ford's sports-racing GT40. The cabin was of monocoque construction while the bonnet and engine cover were made of aluminium and, accordingly, unstressed. Note the cooling ducts for the transversely mounted V12 engine.

Stunning styling by Bertone

These revolutionary mechanicals were cloaked in a stunning Bertone coupé body, the work of 26-year-old Marcello Gandini. The resulting car was displayed at the 1966 Geneva Motor Show where its name was revealed as the Miura. This was in tribute to Don Eduardo Miura, a breeder of fighting bulls – Ferruccio Lamborghini, who was born under the Zodiac sign of Taurus the bull, being drawn to names with taurine associations.

Entering production early in 1967, the Miura was a mere 41in (1041mm) high, and was utterly distinctive and beautifully proportioned with a tail that could be mistaken for no other on account of the innovative engine location.

If you can't stand the heat...

The heat generated by the V12 was a major problem, however, so a series of louvres, that were likened to the slats of a venetian blind, were introduced to permit some rear visibility and, principally, to allow the hot air to escape. However, this meant inserting a window between the cockpit

and engine compartment to separate the occupants from the twin bugbears of high temperature levels and noise.

At the front, the swivelling headlamps were set in what looked suspiciously like eyelashes but which were in fact disguised ducts that directed cooling air to the front brakes.

Top speed was over 170mph (274km/h) and the Miura combined out and out performance with the handling expected from a mid-engined machines.

In 1969 the even more powerful Miura S with 375bhp on tap was unveiled but the ultimate version was the SV of 1971 with 385bhp, wider track and rear wheels and, in consequence, back wings. The original 'eyelashes' were also banished. Destined for a relatively short life, the last SV was built late in 1972. There would be a two-year hiatus before the Miura was replaced by the equally spectacular Countach.

Left above: The Miura's headlights rapidly elevated when they were switched on. The colour of the 'eyelashes' changed with the paint colour.

Left below: The only way in which the V12 could be transversely mounted was to locate the gearbox Mini-style in the sump.

Below: The cockpit was well equipped, but it was a little on the small side and noisy because of the close proximity of the engine.

Specification	Lamborghini Miura
Engine location	Mid, transverse
Configuration	V12
Bore and stroke	82 x 62mm
Capacity	3929cc
Valve operation	Twin overhead camshafts per bank
Horsepower	350bhp @ 7000rpm
Transmission	Manual five-speed
Drive	Rear
Chassis	Steel box section
Suspension – front	Wishbones and coil spring
Suspension – rear	Wishbones and coil spring
Brakes	Disc
Top speed	171mph (274km/h)
Acceleration	0-60mph (0-96km/h): 6 seconds

Ferrari Daytona

Below: *Last of the great front-engined Ferrari berlinettas, for the time being at least, the Daytona's Pininfarina-styled body is regarded as one of the design house's finest creations. The sense of balance between the long bonnet, its lines uninterrupted by projecting headlights, and the relatively small passenger area is outstanding.*

Top speed
174mph
280km/h

Ferrari's first generation of fabled V12-engined berlinettas came to an end in 1973 with the demise of the big and memorable Daytona which was capable of no less than 174mph (280km/h). When the prototype was unveiled at the 1968 Paris Salon, what was then described at the 365 GTB/4 was hailed as the fastest road car in Ferrari's history.

Interestingly, the Daytona name was not an official one but the car was so christened by the press following Ferrari's victory in the 1967 Daytona 24 hour race.

Pininfarina had produced a magnificent and distinctive coupé body in which the headlamps, for aerodynamic considerations, were located behind clear plastic covers within the finely chiselled nose. However, they were subsequently found not to conform to regulations in the all-important American market so retractable units were introduced above the originals.

The seat of power

The long bonnet concealed an all-alloy, 4.4 litre, four-cam, V12 engine; although this followed the layout of Ferrari's earlier power units, it was essentially new in execution. The dry sump unit came complete with six Weber carburettors and it developed an impressive 352bhp. The five-speed ZF gearbox was in unit with the transaxle.

There was the usual tubular chassis with all-independent suspension and disc brakes but this was a heavy car with a long wheelbase and it turned the scales at 3600lb (1633kg).

Although Pininfarina had been responsible for the design and construction of the prototype, the bodies of the production cars, which appeared a year after the model's Paris debut, were built in Modena by Scaglietti. Audaciously, there was only room for two occupants.

Performance and handling was up to Maranello's usual demanding standards. And while the brakes were sufficient for road use, they displayed their limitations on racing versions that were capable of speeds approaching 200mph (321km/h). Examples ran at Le Mans in 1971 and 1972 when Daytonas attained creditable fifth placings on both occasions, and in the latter year also occupied sixth to ninth positions.

A convertible (spider) version of the model was unveiled at the 1969 Frankfurt Motor Show and it also displayed sensational lines. Although the berlinettas inevitably predominated, about 150 open cars were built.

When Daytona production ceased in 1973, some 1350 examples had been completed. It was replaced by the mid-engined 365 GT4BB, the legendary Boxer. But if the public thought that it had seen the last front-engined Ferrari, it was very much mistaken…

Above: Despite the Daytona's size, there is only room for two people; the view down that long bonnet is memorable.

Left: Although the great majority of Daytonas were coupés, there were some convertibles which are greatly sought after.

Below left: Beneath that substantial air cleaner are six Weber carburettors. The twin oil filters are remarkably accessible.

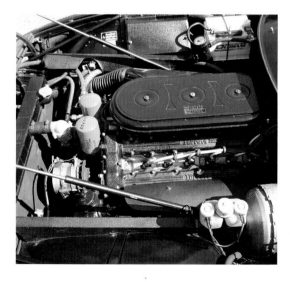

Specification	Ferrari 365 GTB/4 Daytona
Engine location	Front, in-line
Configuration	V12
Bore and stroke	81 x 71mm
Capacity	4390cc
Valve operation	Twin overhead camshafts per bank
Horsepower	352bhp @ 7500rpm
Transmission	Manual five-speed
Drive	Rear
Chassis	Tubular steel
Suspension – front	Wishbones and coil spring
Suspension – rear	Wishbones and coil spring
Brakes	Disc
Top speed	174mph (280km/h)
Acceleration	0-60mph (0-96km/h): 5.4 seconds

Plymouth Road Runner Superbird

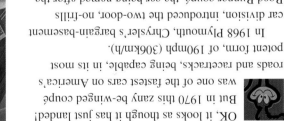

OK, it looks as though it has just landed! But in 1970 this zany be-winged coupé was one of the fastest cars on America's roads and racetracks, being capable, in its most potent form, of 190mph (306km/h).

In 1968 Plymouth, Chrysler's bargain-basement car division, introduced the two-door, no-frills Road Runner coupé, the car being named after the Warner Brothers cartoon character of that name. It even possessed a distinctive beep-beep horn in tribute to its inspiration.

In what was to be dubbed the Muscle Car era, the 'Runner was based on Plymouth's new Belvedere model, and powered by the company's proven 383cid (6.3 litre) V8, enhanced to produce 325bhp. Aimed at the young driver to take to the racetrack, the 'Runner was progressively up-engined, surviving in this form until 1970. In that year its most extreme manifestation was unveiled in the form of the Superbird.

Created to meet NASCAR (National Association for Stock Car Auto Racing) homologation track requirements, the authorities required that no less than 1000 Road Runner Superbirds had to be sold commercially to meet qualification regulations. Plymouth responded that it had orders for 2000 and, in due course, 1971 machines found owners. As such small numbers were involved, aftermarket specialist Creative Industries was responsible for the aerodynamic modifications.

Below: You couldn't mistake it for anything else! The black vinyl roof was a standard fitment, along with the unmissable fixed rear stabilizer, the presence of which did not significantly affect the car's behaviour.

Right: The Superbird was fitted with a 440cid V8 as standard, but there was an optional and even more powerful 426 'hemi' available.

This required extending the front of the car by 18in (457mm) – the resulting chiselled nose incorporated pop-up headlamps behind glass-fibre flaps. The original recessed rear window was replaced by flush-fitting glass but, to hide evidence of this modification, all 'Birds were fitted with a black vinyl roof.

Outlandish spoiler

Much more apparent was a large spoiler mounted some 24in (610mm) above the car's boot with the Road Runner decal featuring on the supports. But despite the 'Bird's outlandish looks, this aerodynamic extension did not prove to be wholly satisfactory. The modifications added weight and didn't really kick in until the Plymouth was travelling at 80 to 90mph (129 to 145km/h).

Most Superbirds were powered by a 375bhp version of the 440cid (7.2 litre) Super Commando V8 with either four-speed manual or TorqueFlite automatic transmission. There was an optional 390hp version and a top line 'hemi' 426cid (7 litre) with 425hp in harness.

While the street cars were good for 140mph (225km/m), those created for the racing circuits only used hemi power and were capable of about 50mph (80km/h) more.

Solely produced for 1970, revised legislation rendered the Superbird obsolete and Plymouth introduced a new Road Runner shape for 1971. Sales of the old line were slow although today they are much sought after by collectors.

Specification	**Plymouth** Road Runnner Superbird
Engine location	Front, in-line
Configuration	V8
Bore and stroke	4.32 x 3.75in (110 x 95mm)
Capacity	440cid (7210cc)
Valve operation	Overhead valve
Horsepower	375bhp @ 4600rpm
Transmission	Manual four-speed
Drive	Rear
Chassis	Unitary
Suspension – front	Wishbones and torsion bar
Suspension – rear	Half-elliptic spring
Brakes	Drum
Top speed	140mph (225km/h)
Acceleration	0-60mph (0-96km/h): 4.9 seconds

Left: The Road Runner cartoon character from which the mainstream model took its name was a 'fun feature' of the car. This cheerful emblem appeared on the spoiler mounts and was repeated on the left-hand headlight flap.

Below: The Superbird's aerodynamically refined nose was made of glass fibre and also incorporated pop-up headlamps.

Lamborghini Countach

Top speed
175mph
282km/h

Replacing a model of the stature of the Miura should have represented a daunting prospect for any car company, but then Lamborghini is no run-of-the-mill motor manufacturer. The new supercar made its debut in 1971 and was named the Countach, a regional North Italian slang word which echoed the appreciative exclamation of a worker when viewing the new car for the first time.

Mid-engined like the Miura, the V12 unit was enlarged to 5 litres, and positioned longitudinally rather than transversely. Chief engineer Paolo Stanzani also dispensed with its predecessor's sump in gearbox design and instead decided to position the five-speed unit in the centre of the car, alongside the driver. But with the drive at the rear it was conveyed, via a sealed tube, within the engine's sump.

Lamborghini once again turned to Bertone's Marcello Gandini to design an appropriate body for these unconventional mechanicals and he did not disappoint. The result was a piece of automotive sculpture of the highest quality, an audacious wedge-shaped coupé with concealed headlamps and memorable upward-opening doors.

Right: *Lamborghini's V12 was mounted longitudinally in the Countach, and in its Diablo successor. However, it was less accessible than the transversely mounted engine in the Miura.*

Below: *The Countach's wedge-shaped profile was made possible by the mid-position of the engine. This is a 400S model of 1981. What appear to be the headlamps are in fact flashing indicators. The real headlamps are of the pop-up variety.*

Enthusiastic reception at launch

The first Countach was completed just in time to be launched at the 1971 Geneva Motor Show where its enthusiastic reception convinced Lamborghini that this was the Miura's true successor. But it was to be a further three years before the first production Countach left the Saint' Agata Bolognese factory in mid-1974. The enlarged V12 had disintegrated during testing so the original 375bhp 3.9 litre unit was reinstated.

Left: Rear view of the 400S. Although the rear spoiler makes a visual contribution to the car, contrary to appearances the Countach does not suffer from aerodynamic lift, and the spoiler adds drag, weight and expense. Note the four exhaust pipes.

Below: A 5000QV bereft of a rear wing and probably the better for it. Outwardly identical to its predecessors, its performance was enhanced by a redesign of the V12 engine which was not only enlarged in capacity but featured four valves per cylinder.

The model was, nevertheless, faster than its predecessor; it could be wound up to about 175mph (282km/h) with 100mph (161km/h) arriving in a little over 13 seconds. And if the driver and passenger found some difficulty in entering or leaving the cockpit, no matter!

The original version survived until 1978 when it was replaced by the Countach S with wider Campagnolo alloy wheels – the arches were flared to accommodate them. A rear wing, which added to the car's aerodynamic aura, became a popular (if not a wholly necessary) extra.

More powerful engine

In 1982 the capacity of the V12 was upped to 4.7 litres and the car was now known as the LP5000S. Further changes were in hand and in 1985 the V12 was not only again increased in capacity, to 5.2 litres, but was also the beneficiary of twin-cam four-valve cylinder heads. Now producing 455bhp, the resulting 5000QV (for *quattrovalvole*) was faster, at 178mph (286km/h), and owners found it easier to drive than its predecessor on account of its torquier engine.

The QV was destined to have a four-year production life. In 1988 Lamborghini released the Anniversary model with mildly revised bodywork which celebrated 25 years as a motor manufacturer. Countach production ceased in July 1990, after a total of 1549 examples had been completed.

Specification	Lamborghini Countach (3.9 litres)
Engine location	Mid, in-line
Configuration	V12
Bore and stroke	82 x 62mm
Capacity	3929cc
Valve operation	Twin overhead camshafts per bank
Horsepower	375bhp @ 8000rpm
Transmission	Manual five-speed
Drive	Rear
Chassis	Tubular steel
Suspension – front	Wishbones and coil spring
Suspension – rear	Wishbones and coil spring
Brakes	Ventilated disc
Top speed	175mph (282km/h)
Acceleration	0-60mph (0-96km/h): 5.7 seconds

Porsche 911 Turbo

Top speed
153mph
246km/h

When Porsche introduced its now legendary 911 in 1962, it was capable of a respectable 130mph (209km/h) top speed. This figure progressively improved over the years but the line received a significant boost in 1974 with the arrival of 911 Turbo that was capable of 153mph (246km/h). It was able to hit 100mph (161km/h) in a mere 14 seconds.

Although Porsche's gargantuan Le Mans-winning 917 sports racer of 1970/l had been further enhanced by a turbocharged engine, the concept had not been immediately extended to road cars. It fell to BMW to introduce, in 1973, the 2002 Turbo, which was Europe's first such street-ready model. Driven by the need to homologate its projected 935 racer in Group 4 competition, Porsche proceeded with a turbocharged version of the 911 that appeared at the 1974 Paris Motor Show.

Tea-tray spoiler

Developed under the 930 designation, the 911 Turbo was instantly identifiable by its wider wheels and accompanying flared arches while there was a large 'tea-tray' spoiler at the rear which helped to keep the back wheels firmly on the road.

Beneath was a mildly tamed race-bred, 3 litre, RSR Carrera, KKK turbocharged, six-cylinder, horizontally opposed, air-cooled engine. In this form it developed 260bhp, a good 60bhp more than the unblown 3 litre Carrera.

Fast but surprisingly flexible, the 911 Turbo was a comfortable, well-appointed car with air conditioning and electric windows fitted as standard. It was produced in this form until 1978 when the engine's capacity was increased to 3.3 litres and a competition-proven intercooler was also introduced which boosted the efficiency of the

Below: Something special: a 1980 3.3 litre Turbo with no chrome apparent, matt black being something of a Porsche speciality! The wider wheels and enhanced arches were established Turbo features by then. Less apparent is the presence of drilled brake discs arrested by Alcon four-piston calipers.

turbocharger. Top speed was increased to 160mph (257km/h) while 100mph (161km/h) could be spirited up in a mere 12 seconds, which made this Turbo the fastest-accelerating road car of its day. Originally fitted with a four-speed gearbox, it was not until 1988 that an extra top cog arrived. This second generation Turbo was built until mid-1989, only to reappear in the spring of 1990 in revised Carrera 2 form.

The third generation Carrera Turbo arrived for 1994 with a 3.6 litre engine, twin KKK turbochargers and four-wheel-drive. Accordingly sure-footed, identifiable by a distinctive howl and exceptionally rapid, it was capable of an impressive 178mph (286km/h).

The current 911 Turbo, introduced for the 2001 season, is similarly driven, has a water-cooled engine and is also available with Tiptronic semi-automatic transmission. And its top speed nudges the 190mph (306km/h) mark…

Left: The 911 Turbo's air-conditioned interior was particularly well appointed. The revolution counter dominated the instrument display and was mounted right in front of the driver with the turbocharger boost gauge set into the bottom of the dial.

Below left: This 3.3 litre Turbo was easily distinguished by the new squared-off rear spoiler with its upturned rubber surround. In addition to generating downforce, it also housed the air-conditioning radiator and served the newly introduced intercooler which reduced the temperature of the turbocharged air and so improved engine efficiency.

Specification	Porsche 911 Turbo (3 litres)
Engine location	Rear, in-line
Configuration	Turbocharged horizontally opposed six-cylinder
Bore and stroke	95 x 70mm
Capacity	2993cc
Valve operation	Single overhead camshaft
Horsepower	260bhp @ 5500rpm
Transmission	Manual four-speed
Drive	Rear
Chassis	Unitary
Suspension – front	Wishbones and torsion bar
Suspension – rear	Semi trailing arm and torsion bar
Brakes	Ventilated disc
Top speed	153mph (246km/h)
Acceleration	0-60mph (0-96km/h): 6.4 seconds

Lotus Esprit Turbo

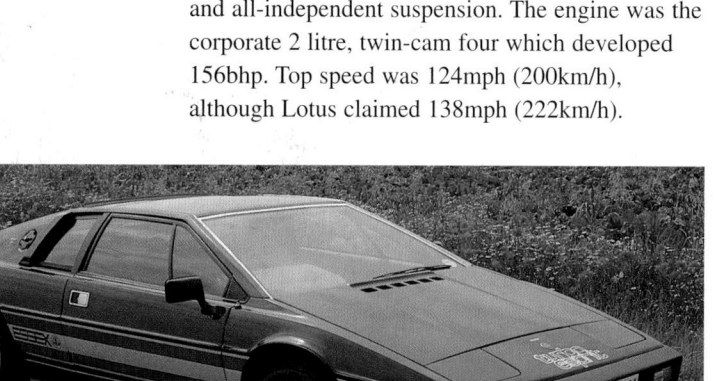

**Top speed
175mph**
282km/h

Lotus's Esprit dates from 1975. It has stylistically and mechanically evolved over the past quarter century, and it can still show a clean pair of heels to most of the opposition with a top speed of 175mph (282km/h).

The result of a fruitful dialogue in 1972 between Lotus's founder, Colin Chapman, and Giorgetto Giugiaro of the Turin-based Ital Design, the Esprit was launched at the 1975 London Motor Show, as a mid-engined, crisply styled, glass-fibre-bodied coupé with Lotus's familiar backbone chassis and all-independent suspension. The engine was the corporate 2 litre, twin-cam four which developed 156bhp. Top speed was 124mph (200km/h), although Lotus claimed 138mph (222km/h).

An engine enlargement to 2.2 litres followed in 1980 and the Esprit Turbo arrived later that year. With 210bhp on tap, it was capable of 150mph (241km/h). The chassis had been redesigned to accept a new V8 engine then under development, although there would be a long wait for this unit.

The 1988 season saw the sharpness of Giugiaro's lines skilfully softened by the company's Peter Stevens. Later, in 1993, came a new nose and tail, power steering and suspension revisions and a supplementary model, the Sport 300 (which reflected its bhp) with a larger turbocharger and wider wheels. This was followed in 1994 by the S4S with the Sport's mechanicals and a luxurious interior.

High performance league

Eventually, in 1996, the Esprit received its long-awaited 3.5 litre V8 engine which developed 349bhp with the aid of twin Garrett T25 turbochargers. At a stroke the model entered a new performance league with top speed soaring to over 175mph (282km/h) and 62mph (100km/h) arriving in a mere 4.5 seconds. However, the blown four-cylinder version remained in production as an entry-level 2 litre GT3, a model that survived, despite all the odds, until 1999.

Above: The Esprit Turbo in its original guise (in Essex Racing colours) sporting the Giugiaro-styled body dating from the model's 1975 introduction. Both wheels and brakes were uprated for the blown version.

Right: The Turbo received its long-awaited V8 engine in 1996, the model having had a visual facelift in 1988. Outwardly similar to its four-cylinder predecessor, this mid-engined Lotus offers praiseworthy performance and handling, although with specifications rooted in the 1970s.

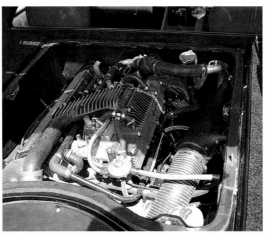

Far left: The badge is the give-away, particularly as the four continued in production.

Left: What treasure lurks under the rear deck – the longitudinally mounted turbocharged four.

Below: The Turbo acquired this new highly distinctive dashboard for the 1998 season.

For 1998 Lotus offered a bargain-basement Esprit, the GT, for a shade under £50,000 – £10,000 less than the original. Bereft of such items as the rear wing and air conditioning, both it and the Esprit V8 received a new roomier interior and fascia.

The 1999 season saw the arrival of the supplementary Sport 350 – the most extreme Esprit ever – which was 176lb (80kg) lighter than the mainstream model. Production was limited to just 50 cars. Easily identifiable by its carbon-fibre rear wing, there were lightweight wheels and suspension and brake uprates. The interior featured carbon fibre and alloy in abundance.

So the Esprit continues to soldier on, but it is now showing its years. The end of the story cannot be far away, can it?

Specification	Lotus Esprit Turbo (3.5 litre)
Engine location	Mid, in-line
Configuration	Twin turbocharged V8
Bore and stroke	81 x 83mm
Capacity	3506cc
Valve operation	Twin overhead camshafts per bank
Horsepower	349bhp @ 6500rpm
Transmission	Manual five-speed
Drive	Rear
Chassis	Backbone
Suspension – front	Wishbones and coil spring
Suspension – rear	Upper and lower link and coil spring
Brakes	Disc
Top speed	175mph (282km/h)
Acceleration	0-62mph (100km/h): 4.5 seconds

Porsche 959

Top speed 197mph 317km/h

It is the ultimate 911. Beneath those familiar body lines are a mind-blowing array of electro/mechanical gizmos which made the 959, for a time, the world's fastest production road car with a top speed of 197mph (317km/h).

Above all, the 959 was a reaffirmation by its makers of the spirit of the 911, with its unorthodox rear-mounted, air-cooled, flat-six engine. The 911 had taken a back seat between 1972-80, when Dr Ernst Fuhrmann was Porsche's chief executive and he decreed a switch to conventional front-engined cars such as the 928. But with the arrival of his successor, Peter Schutz, the 911 once again moved centre stage and it has remained there ever since.

Porsche unveiled its four-wheel-drive *Gruppe B* car at the 1983 Frankfurt Motor Show. Aimed at Group B competition, this required that a minimum of 200 be produced for homologation purposes. Power came from a special 2.8 litre twin-turbocharged version of the 911's air-cooled flat-six engine which had competition-proven water-cooled cylinder heads.

Right: Only produced in left-hand-drive form, the 959's interior shows some similarity to the 911 Turbo's. Despite its sophistication, this Porsche also has the virtue of being remarkably easy to drive.

Below: A 959 doing what it does best: travelling at speed. The relationship with the 911 is readily apparent. The air intakes are to help keep the massive discs cool.

This element of what was to be designated the 959 was resolved relatively quickly. Unfortunately the complex four-wheel-drive system took longer to develop than expected and the first example did not reach its patient customer until April 1987, three and a half years after the model was announced.

In the meantime an early version of the car had proved its worth on the demanding Paris to Dakar rally which it won in 1984. A further success followed in 1986. However, in that year, Group B, for which the 959 had been so carefully tailored, was banned in the wake of a series of fatal crashes.

Well worth waiting for

When the definitive 959 appeared, it proved well worth the wait. Deceptively easy to drive, at the heart of the four-wheel-drive system was the computer-controlled Porsche Control Clutch which distributed the correct amount of torque between the front and rear wheels.

For fast motoring, Porsche claimed a top speed of 193mph (311km/h); in fact 197mph (317km/h) was attainable when on-board computer control lowered the body to within 4.9in (124mm) of the ground. But uneven road surfaces could be accommodated with a 5.9in (150mm) setting and the car could be electrically jacked up to 7in (178mm) if the need arose.

Only produced in left-hand-drive form, demand was such that Porsche eventually produced 250 cars, 50 more than it had intended, the last example being delivered in 1988.

Specification	Porsche 959
Engine location	Rear, in-line
Configuration	Twin turbocharged horizontally opposed six-cylinder
Bore and stroke	95 x 67mm
Capacity	2849cc
Valve operation	Twin overhead camshafts per bank
Horsepower	450bhp @ 6500rpm
Transmission	Manual six-speed
Drive	Four wheel
Chassis	Unitary
Suspension – front	Wishbones and coil spring
Suspension – rear	Wishbones and coil spring
Brakes	Ventilated disc
Top speed	197mph (317km/h)
Acceleration	0-60mph (96km/h): 3.6 seconds

Left: Much of the 959's 2.8 litre, flat-six turbocharged engine cannot be seen when the lid is raised.

Below: The fixed rear spoiler helps to keep the engine's 450 horsepower on the road.

Ferrari F40

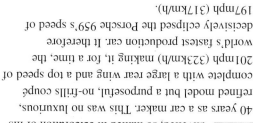

**Top speed
201 mph
323km/h**

Enzo Ferrari produced his first cars in 1947. In 1987 the F40 supercar was unveiled, so named in celebration of his 40 years as a car maker. This was no luxurious, refined model but a purposeful, no-frills coupé complete with a large rear wing and a top speed of 201mph (323km/h) making it, for a time, the world's fastest production car. It therefore decisively eclipsed the Porsche 959's speed of 197mph (317km/h).

Based on the floorpan of the 288 GTO of 1984, the F40 was powered by a related twin turbocharged V8 engine of a mere 3 litres capacity, although it developed a stupendous 478bhp. It was rear-mounted in a longitudinal position.

Weight-saving was an overriding consideration, and although a tubular space-frame chassis, which provided the outline of the cabin and tail sections, was retained, extensive use was made of Kevlar and carbon fibre. Both materials came courtesy of Ferrari's Formula 1 activities.

While Pininfarina had ultimate responsibility for the styling, the F40's body was produced at Maranello by Ferrari.

Kevlar and glass-fibre body panels also featured, and further kilograms were saved in the cockpit which was bereft of such niceties as carpeting and door trim. In consequence the F40 turned the scales at just 2425lb (1100kg).

Right: Function rather than creature comfort is the keynote of a 1991 F40. Weight-saving was a consideration – note the drilled pedals.

Below: This is a pre-production Ferrari F40 of 1988. The sliding perspex windows are wholly in keeping with the model's racing pedigree although they were subsequently replaced by glass.

Three suspension settings

The all-independent suspension used the customary Ferrari wishbones and coil springs and there were no less than three settings – normal, high speed which involved lowering it by 0.75in (19 mm), and parking when it was raised by the same amount.

Although outwardly resembling a road car, the acceleration was phenomenal – this most exclusive of Ferraris was able to reach 200km/h (124mph) in a mere 12 seconds.

If for some reason you were not satisfied with this level of performance, for several million lire Ferrari would extract a further 200bhp from the trusty V8. Needless to say noise levels within the sparsely furnished cockpit made speech between driver and passenger virtually impossible. But then no one ever bought an F40 to hold conversations in!

Production began early in 1988. The F40 was priced in Britain at £193,299, some £80,000 more that its Testarossa stablemate. It remained in production until 1992; although it had been intended to restrict production to just 450 cars, worldwide demand for the model remained strong

Specification	Ferrari F40
Engine location	Rear, in-line
Configuration	Twin turbocharged V8
Bore and stroke	82 x 69mm
Capacity	2936cc
Valve operation	Twin overhead camshafts per bank
Horsepower	478bhp @ 7000rpm
Transmission	Manual five-speed
Drive	Four wheel
Chassis	Tubular steel, Kevlar and carbon fibre
Suspension – front	Wishbones and coil spring
Suspension – rear	Wishbones and coil spring
Brakes	Ventilated discs
Top speed	201mph (323km/h)
Acceleration	0-60mph (0-96 km/h): 4.7 seconds

and eventually nearly three times that number, 1311 F40s no less, had been completed before production ceased in 1992.

It had been an extraordinarily impressive car, daring and distinctive. Perversely, the even faster F50 appeared in 1995, two years *before* the marque celebrated its half century!

Above: The F40's unmistakable rear view; its body was made of race-proven fibreglass, Kevlar and carbon fibre. This is a 1990 car with conventional side windows.

Lamborghini Diablo

With a top speed in excess of just over 202mph (325km/h), Lamborghini's Diablo just pipped the Ferrari F40 as the world's fastest car, that is until the Jaguar XJ220 came along in 1991.

The Miura and Countach had established Lamborghini's reputation for creating stunning flagship supercars and while the Diablo effectively inherited the latter's mechanicals, the durable V12 was further enlarged, this time to 5.7 litres, with 485bhp on tap.

With a wheelbase 7.9in (200mm) longer than the Countach's, the coupé body was clearly derived from it. It was the work of Marcello Gandini, no longer with Bertone but now freelance, who was responsible for the styling of both the Diablo's illustrious predecessors. It did, however, lack some of the impact of his earlier work.

After some input from Chrysler, Lamborghini's owner in the years 1987 to 1994, the car was launched at Monte Carlo in January 1990. But in typical Lamborghini style, production did not begin until a year later, at the height of a world recession.

The world's fastest car

The company's claim of a top speed of 202mph (325km/h) and a 0 to 100km/h (62mph) figure of 4.9 seconds was subsequently confirmed by the American *Road & Track* magazine which attained 202.33mph (325.60mph), just 1.33mph (2.1km/h) quicker than Ferrari's F40. But its accolade as the world's fastest car proved to be short-lived with the launch, in October 1991, of the Jaguar XJ220 which could exceed 213mph (343km/h).

Right: In 1993 Lamborghini announced the 30SE, built to commemorate the company's 30th anniversary in 1994. Power was upped to 525bhp but rear visibility was not its strongest point!

Below: The Diablo, this example dates from 1990, is clearly derived from its Countach predecessor, although perhaps it lacks the visual impact. It has endured for 11 years and has progressively improved during this production span.

Top speed
202mph
325km/h

Left: A 1999 Diablo with its aluminium bodywork replaced by lighter, stronger carbon fibre. Arguably the best built model to date and a reflection of Volkswagen's ownership of Lamborghini.

Below left: The Diablo's instrument panel has much to commend it for functional appeal. The gear lever sits, Ferrari-like, in an open visible gate.

Improved aerodynamics

While the Diablo handled as you might expect a mid-engined car to do, its lack of power steering and anti-lock brakes were clear deficiencies. Four-wheel-drive was another but all these shortcomings were remedied in 1993 with the arrival of the Diablo VT, standing for Viscous Traction FWD. Then, for 1994, came the Diablo SE, for Special Edition, with a wildly optimistic claimed top speed of 220mph (354km/h), improved aerodynamics and engine power boosted to 525bhp.

In 1996 came the lightweight SV, which stood for Sport Veloce, with 'only' 508bhp on tap. The same year saw the arrival of the long-awaited convertible version also with four-wheel-drive. Much of the styling was reworked and the detachable Targa-style roof stored externally behind the driver.

Although Lamborghini has been owned by Volkswagen since 1998, the Diablo's replacement has enjoyed a typically lengthy gestation. In the meantime the fastest-ever Lamborghini, the Diablo

GT, was unveiled in 2000 with a claimed top speed of 210mph (338km/h). The aluminium bodywork was replaced by carbon fibre which helped to reduce weight by 198lb (90kg). A 585bhp 6 litre engine arrived for 2001, which, after 11 years, was destined to be the final year of Diablo production.

Above: The long-heralded Diablo roadster appeared in 1996. Much of the bodywork was reworked, and the roof is carried outboard above the engine.

Specification	Lamborghini Diablo VT
Engine location	Mid, in-line
Configuration	V12
Bore and stroke	87 x 80mm
Capacity	5707cc
Valve operation	Twin overhead camshafts per bank
Horsepower	485bhp @ 7000rpm
Transmission	Manual five-speed
Drive	Four-wheel
Chassis	Tubular steel
Suspension – front	Wishbones and coil spring
Suspension – rear	Wishbones and coil spring
Brakes	Ventilated disc
Top speed	202mph (325km/h)
Acceleration	0-62mph (0-100km/h): 4.1 seconds

Vauxhall Lotus Carlton

Apart from a rear spoiler and a couple of air intakes let into the bonnet, there was little outwardly to signal the difference between a Lotus Carlton and the mainstream five-seater family model on which it was based. But with a claimed top speed of 176mph (283km/h) it was, in 1990, the world's fastest saloon car.

Introduced in 1986, the Carlton was the Vauxhall version of the German-built and designed Opel Rekord, both makes having been owned since the 1920s by the American General Motors Corporation. More recently, in 1986, GM had acquired British sports car manufacturer and engineering consultant Lotus, and this concern was responsible not only for effecting the important modifications but also for completing the model's assembly. Announced at the 1989 Geneva Motor Show, this BMW-beater did not enter production until late in 1990 and it was also badged as the Opel Lotus Omega in Europe.

Developing no less than 377bhp, the engine was based on the 3 litre unit used in Vauxhall's flagship Carlton GSi. Possessing unique 95 x 85mm internal dimensions, which gave 3615cc, it was fitted with an aluminium twin-overhead-camshaft four-valve cylinder head. The turbochargers were twin Garrett T25 units, each with its own water-cooled intercooler. There was a phenomenal 419lb/ft of torque.

Right: The Lotus Carlton's rear spoiler was far from just decorative – it helped to keep the rear wheels firmly on the road.

Below: The front spoiler with its substantial air intakes, widened wheel arches and Ronal alloy wheels distinguished this model. The drag coefficient was a creditable 0.31.

Top speed
176mph
283km/h

Left: The interior was another departure from the norm with leather upholstered seats supplying plenty of side support, although the rears were bucket-style. The steering wheel was adjustable for rake and the speedometer read to 180mph (290km/h).

Below: A bonnetful of engine! The great virtue of this twin turbocharged 3.6 litre V6 was its flexibility with a broad power band and no less than 377bhp on tap. Lotus had done its work well.

Drive was taken via a six-speed ZF gearbox, similar to that used on the in-house Chevrolet Corvette, to a strengthened differential. Further departures from standard were modestly uprated suspension, substantial 12.5in (317mm) ventilated all-round disc brakes with racing calipers and massive Ronal alloy wheels.

Connolly leather interior

The interior was also peculiar to the model, being trimmed throughout in Connolly leather hide with fully supportive sports front seats, each of which contained an electronic 'memory'. Electric windows and sunroof also featured.

In total nine pre-production cars were built and testing was undertaken at the Nardo high-speed circuit in southern Italy where speeds of 176mph (283km/h) were achieved. Vauxhall optimistically spoke of 180mph (290km/h) being possible. However, this prompted controversy and corporate advertisements made no mention of its potential top speed, only its impressive 0-60mph (0-96km/h) figure of 5.2 seconds.

GM envisaged making 1100 cars over three years. While it sold for a competitive £48,000, the model, alas, ran into the recession of the early 1990s. While Lotus completed them at an initial rate of 13 a week, production was curtailed a year early in December 1992. In all 950 were completed, 150 short of the original figure, with the Carlton accounting for 320 and the balance of 630 given over to the Opel version.

Specification	Vauxhall Lotus Carlton
Engine location	Front, in-line
Configuration	Twin turbocharged six-cylinder
Bore and stroke	95 x 85mm
Capacity	3615cc
Valve operation	Twin overhead camshafts
Horsepower	377bhp @ 5200rpm
Transmission	Manual six-speed
Drive	Rear
Chassis	Unitary
Suspension – front	MacPherson strut and coil spring
Suspension – rear	Multi link, semi trailing arm and coil spring
Brakes	Ventilated disc
Top speed	176mph (283km/h)
Acceleration	0-60mph (0-96km/h: 5.2 seconds

Dodge Viper

**Top speed
172mph**
277km/h

*Right: Simplicity is the
essential theme of the Viper
and this is no more
apparent than in the no-
frills cockpit. The seats are
supportive and boast
inflatable lumbar control.
Legroom is also good.*

*Below: Although only
produced in left-hand-drive
form, the car is sold in
Europe as the Chrysler
Viper because the Dodge
name is used on a French
truck. It has the virtue of
looking good when viewed
from any angle.*

500/500/500. These figures alluringly stand for brake horsepower, pounds/feet of torque, and (in truth) approximate cubic inches, and they are being used as a marketing formula to promote the second generation Dodge Viper that is due to hit the streets of its native America in August 2002.

It has been a remarkable success story for the hunky no-frills two-seater that began life as a concept car back at the 1989 Detroit Motor Show. Created for Dodge's Chrysler parent by Carroll Shelby, who was responsible for the 1960s AC Cobra (hence the related Viper name), this unashamedly 'back to basics' concept of an open two-seater was powered by an overhead-valve V10 engine intended for the next generation of Chrysler trucks and sports utilities.

Such was its reception at the show, Chrysler decided to put this unconventional Dodge into production. The body, with its steel centre section and glass-fibre nose and tail and replete with Ferrari, Jaguar and Cobra echoes, was retained essentially intact, but the power unit did require some modification.

Aluminium engine block

Revamped by in-house Lamborghini, the original cast-iron block was replaced by an aluminium one; changes to the combustion chamber and valve gear produced a unit that developed 400bhp, a 100bhp improvement on the original. The red rocker boxes were Ferrari-inspired. The exhaust outlet of drainpipe-like proportions emerged from an exposed silencer just below the passenger's door.

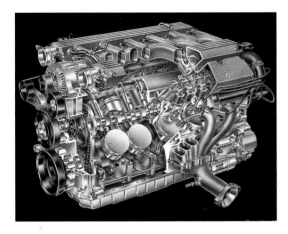

Above left: Inside the Viper's V10 engine that began life as a truck unit and was reworked by in-house Lamborghini in aluminium. A big, low-revving 8 litre, overhead valve actuation was via hydraulic tappets and pushrods.

Above right: The way forward. Chrysler's GTS/R concept Viper of 2000 forms the basis of the next generation of cars. It is longer, wider and lower than the original.

Left: Although the Viper began life as an open two-seater, a coupé version was inevitable, the GTS being unveiled in 1993. This profile underlines the success of the conversion which looks like a new model in its own right.

Entering production in 1992, Chrysler claimed a top speed of 165mph (266km/h) with 60mph (96km/h) arriving in a raucous and exceedingly rapid 4.5 seconds.

The 1993 Los Angeles Motor Show witnessed the appearance of a coupé version – the GTS, at it was titled, used a more powerful 450bhp engine. Lighter than the open car and more aerodynamically efficient, it was also noticeably faster and able to attain over 170mph (274km/h). As with the roadster, there was a gap, in this instance three years, before the first production version GTS reached its customers during 1996.

In the meantime the roadster was being up-gunned and the 550bhp Venom was followed in 1997 by the Venom 600 with no less than 635bhp on tap.

Chrysler sprung another surprise at the 2000 Detroit show when it unveiled the Viper GTS/R concept coupé and it in turn inspired the '03 season version that made its surprise debut at the 2001 Detroit event. The RT-10 Convertible is an open car like the original, and most noticeably it inherited the concept's distinctive sculptured side panels.

Specification	Dodge Viper GTS
Engine location	Front, in-line
Configuration	V10
Bore and stroke	4 x 3.85in (101 x 98mm)
Capacity	487cid (7990cc)
Valve operation	Pushrod
Horsepower	378bhp @ 5100rpm
Transmission	Manual six-speed
Drive	Rear
Chassis	Tubular
Suspension – front	Wishbones and coil spring
Suspension – rear	Wishbones and coil spring
Brakes	Disc
Top speed	172mph (277km/h)
Acceleration	0-60mph (0-96km/h): 5.3 seconds

It is 0.7in (18mm) shorter and lighter than the present version but with a 2.5in (66mm) longer wheelbase. The V10's capacity has been increased to 8.3 litres, actually 505cid, and Chrysler is hoping that the recurring 500 theme will prove irresistible to potential customers, and is aiming the car at an even wider public than the original.

Jaguar XJ220

Between the autumn of 1991 and the end of 1993, the Jaguar XJ220, with a top speed of 213mph (343km/h), was the world's fastest production car. That was until the arrival of the McLaren F1...

The starting point of what was really a very un-Jaguar-like project came in December 1984 when the company's director of engineering, Jim Randle, inspired by Porsche's 959, began thinking in terms of a 500bhp Jaguar supercar. This would be powered by a non-standard version of the corporate V12, a 6.2 litre unit with twin overhead camshafts and four-valve cylinder heads, rather than the usual 5.3 litre single cam/two-valve ones.

With engineers volunteering their labour and working on Saturday mornings, it took nearly four years to bring the project to fruition. The completed mid-engined silver coupé was unveiled at the 1988 Birmingham Motor Show. Clad in a stunning body styled by Jaguar's Keith Helfer, complete with scissor doors and with a host of refinements, it had a theoretical top speed of over 200mph (321km/h).

Decision to proceed

Although Jaguar was acquired by Ford in 1989, the new management decided to proceed with the project and announced that 350 examples of a simplified XJ220 would be built at a cost of £361,000 each, which was about twice the price of a Ferrari F40. The new version was unveiled in October 1991 at the Tokyo Motor Show but the world was by then in a deepening recession.

Eight inches (203mm) shorter than the Birmingham Show car and shorn of its V12 engine, scissor doors, four-wheel drive, adaptive suspension and anti-lock brakes, the coupé nevertheless outwardly resembled the original. Under the rear decking was a stubbier (but no less potent) twin turbocharged 3.5 litre V6 engine which developed an astounding 524bhp. The top speed was a world-beating 213mph (343km/h) and 100mph (161km/h) arriving in an eye-blinking eight seconds.

Below: If the XJ220's mechanical specification was a simplified version of that of the original show car, the body lines were stunning and bore no resemblance to any other roadgoing model. This example is finished in Silverstone Silver. Five metallic finishes were available to customers, mostly in darker hues.

Right: The XJ220's lines are stunning and it also has the virtue of being easy to drive at high speed. Unlike the 1988 show car, this model has conventional doors rather than the memorable upward-opening variety. The rear wing is barely noticeable.

Top speed 213mph 343km/h

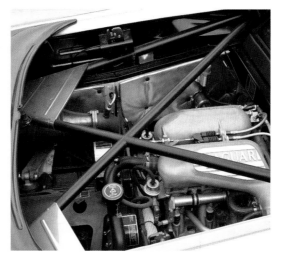

Far left: The 220's interior was not over-elaborate but was commended for its excellent driving position and body-hugging seats. The door-mounted dials were a novel feature.

Left: Around half the length of the original show car's V12, the deceptively small V6 packed a considerable punch, although critics were disappointed by its exhaust note.

12 per cent price rise

Unfortunately the 220's price had risen by some 12 per cent, to £403,000, and a number of prospective customers who had paid a £50,000 deposit found in the chill of 1991 that they were unable to complete the order.

There was also a lightened version, the XJ220-C of 1993. A trio of these cars entered that year's Le Mans 24 hour race and one example won the GT class, although it was subsequently disqualified on a technicality.

But the project continued to be overshadowed by controversy and in the event the projected production figure of 350 was cut to 275. The last car was completed in the spring of 1994.

Specification	Jaguar XJ220
Engine location	Mid, in-line
Configuration	Twin turbocharged V6
Bore and stroke	94 x 84mm
Capacity	3498cc
Valve operation	Twin overhead camshafts per bank
Horsepower	542bhp @ 7200rpm
Transmission	Manual five-speed
Drive	Rear
Chassis	Bonded aluminium honeycomb
Suspension – front	Wishbones and coil spring
Suspension – rear	Wishbones and coil spring
Brakes	Ventilated disc
Top speed	213mph (343km/h)
Acceleration	0-60mph (0-96km/h): 4 seconds

The V12/gearbox unit was attached directly to a central monocoque tub and here Formula 1 input was immediately apparent as it was built up from

The power unit was a longitudinally mounted purpose-designed 6 litre BMW V12 with twin-cam cylinder heads. Drive went to the rear wheels (rather than all four which was the fashion) via a six-speed gearbox. With 550bhp on tap the brakes were four-caliper racing-type Brembo units.

Although it appeared back in 1993, the fabulous McLaren F1 with a top speed of 240mph (386km/h) still bears the mantle of the world's fastest production car.

McLaren is, of course, better known as the manufacturer of Formula 1 single-seaters. It was in the early 1990s that its chief designer, Gordon Murray, who had long harboured the desire to produce 'the ultimate road car', was given the corporate green light to proceed. Murray was in the enviable position of being able to design what could only be named the F1 from a clean sheet of paper. There would be no components carried over from any other models and racing car technology would feature prominently in its specification.

Aerodynamic styling

McLaren was also fortunate to secure the services of stylist Peter Stevens, and his aerodynamically efficient rakish coupé with its two distinctive scissor doors complemented perfectly Murray's mid-engined mechanicals.

Below: A hidden refinement was fan-assisted underfloor aerodynamics intended to extract the maximum performance from the F1. Even the electric mirrors were wind-tunnel tested!

Right: A unique seating position for a special type of road car. In the F1 the driver sits forward of the two passenger seats which are located either side of him, or her.

**Top speed
240mph** 386km/h

McLaren F1

no less than 94 sections of carbon fibre, aluminium and honeycomb which were then oven-baked in McLaren's own facility.

When the F1 was unveiled on the night prior to the 1993 Monaco Grand Prix, which was appropriately won by McLaren, the company announced that just 300 F1s would be built priced at £540,000 apiece. This worked out at £180,000 per occupant because the McLaren was not a two- but a three seater. Unusually the driver sat centrally, the red upholstered seat being set forward of the others. Once so ensconced, the lucky individual would be in charge of one of the fastest, and safest, cars on the road.

With such a pedigree it was natural that the F1 would soon gravitate to the racetrack. The competition GTR version of 1994 was lighter, and with its power upped to a restricted 630bhp it won the 1995 and 1996 GT Championships. It also triumphed at Le Mans in 1995 when these extraordinary McLarens took first, third, fourth, fifth and thirteenth places. In celebration a handful of 668bhp LM F1s were built. The ultimate GT of 1997 was longer and wider than the original but only eight were produced.

Despite the mouth-watering specifications, demand for the F1 never reached the expected levels and only 100 had been completed by the time production ceased at the end of 1997.

Specification	McLaren F1
Engine location	Mid, in-line
Configuration	V12
Bore and stroke	86 x 87mm
Capacity	6064cc
Valve operation	Twin overhead camshafts per bank
Horsepower	627bhp @ 7400rpm
Transmission	Manual six-speed
Drive	Rear
Chassis	Carbon-fibre monocoque
Suspension – front	Wishbones and coil spring
Suspension – rear	Wishbones and coil spring
Brakes	Ventilated discs
Top speed	240mph (386km/h)
Acceleration	0-60mph (0-96km/h): 3.2 seconds

Left: A bespoke 6 litre BMW V12 even if the covers, that conceal twin overhead camshafts, are marked McLaren. The exhaust system incorporates four catalytic converters.

Below: Open wide! The efficiency of the brakes can be taken as read, the discs being arrested by light alloy four-piston calipers.

Ferrari F50

**Top speed
202mph**
325km/h

Opposite top: The F50 body is built entirely of race-proven carbon fibre and the material also features in the central monocoque tub around which the car is built up. Like the McLaren, the rear wheels are wider than the fronts.

Below: The view as one overtakes you! The Ferrari badge on the front wing leaves you in no doubt as to this car's pedigree. Note the break in the rear wing line, the rear section of the body hinges at this point.

Although Ferrari celebrated its 50th anniversary in 1997, the commemorative F50 arrived prematurely in 1995. While outwardly resembling a 1970s sports racer, at its heart was one of the company's successful Formula 1 racing cars re-vamped for the road.

The fastest and most powerful Ferrari of its day, it was based on the 641 series single-seater in which Alain Prost won six races during the 1990 season. Like so many of its contemporaries, the F50 was built up around a central tub with a Nomex honeycomb core skinned in epoxy resin-bonded carbon fibre. Most of this was concealed by the bodywork, but the material was also outwardly apparent, being used for the body panels, seats and even the gearlever knob.

Strong retro styling

The Pininfarina-styled body, that was produced in coupé (with and without a detachable roof) and open forms, displayed strong retro influences while the big fixed rear wing was an obligatory fitment. Both turbocharging and four-wheel drive were eschewed. Unlike the F40 which had used a blown V8 engine, the F50 was powered by a mid-located, longitudinally mounted, 4.7 litre V12 that evolved from the racer's 3.5 litre unit. Developing 513bhp,

the 109.2bhp per litre made the F50 the most powerful normally aspirated supercar of its day. In consequence it was able to reach 60mph (96km/h) in a blistering 3.7 seconds and could attain 202mph (325km/h), just 1mph (1.6km/h) faster than its no-frills F40 predecessor.

Drive was taken by a new six-speed gearbox, although a conventional gate, rather than the usual steering wheel-mounted push button changes, was used. The combined unit was bolted directly to the rear bulkhead.

Instrumentation consisted, in essence, of just a rev counter and speedometer. In line with Formula 1 practice, the blue-hued dials were liquid crystal displays on which the needles only appeared when the ignition was switched on.

Suspension was a compliant system which rapidly responded to road conditions via an electronic control unit. The car's construction was very weight-conscious, and the complete vehicle turned the scales at a respectable 2712lb (1230kg). But relating a road car so closely to Formula 1 technology produced its own problems because noise – the result of shackling the V12, gearbox and rear suspension directly to the cockpit – proved to be an insuperable obstacle.

Ferrari engineers therefore recognized that customers would have to live with the concept of a racer only mildly tamed for the highways of the world. Production was set at 349 cars and exactly that number was completed by the time the last example appeared on 30 July 1997, the year in which Ferrari celebrated its half centenary.

Left: This could be a shot of the engine of a Formula 1 Ferrari, and the F50's is similarly a dry-sump unit. The twin cam heads are made of aluminium although the V12 block is of cast iron. There are no less than five valves per cylinder, three inlet and two exhaust.

Specification	Ferrari F50
Engine location	Mid, in-line
Configuration	V12
Bore and stroke	85 x 69mm
Capacity	4698cc
Valve operation	Twin overhead camshafts per bank
Horsepower	513bhp @ 8000rpm
Transmission	Manual six-speed
Drive	Rear
Chassis	Carbon-fibre composite monocoque
Suspension – front	Wishbones, pushrod and coil spring
Suspension – rear	Wishbones, pushrod and coil spring
Brakes	Ventilated disc
Top speed	202mph (325km/h)
Acceleration	0-60mph (0-96km/h): 3.7 seconds

Jaguar XKR

Right: Although the XK8 on which the R is based can be regarded as the E-Type's successor, it is a much more refined product and is only available with automatic transmission.

Below: The Jaguar XKR is distinguished by its meshed radiator grille that is similar to that on the XJR saloon which shares the same 4 litre supercharged engine. Note the absence of bumpers.

Top speed
155mph*
249km/h
*Limited

The XKR, which Jaguar claims is its fastest-accelerating car, can reach 60mph (96km/h) in just 5.2 seconds. It made its debut at the 1998 Geneva Motor Show. That was two years after the XK8, on which it is based.

Available in coupé and convertible forms which revealed plenty of visual reminders of its famous E-Type forebear, the XK8 of 1996 was an all-new car powered by a 4 litre, 290bhp, V8 twin-cam engine that was making its debut in the model. However, refinement was the order of the day because it was only available with five-speed automatic transmission courtesy of Mercedes-Benz.

The engine was subsequently extended to the existing XJ6 saloon which was accordingly transformed into the XJ8 for the 1998 season. A new XJR supercharged version, in which the V8 was enhanced by the fitment of a Eaton M112 blower boosting output to 370bhp, was capable of a limited 155mph (249Km/h) top speed and was able to hit 60mph (96km/h) figure in 5.3 seconds.

50th anniversary

The similarly upgunned XKR followed at the 1998 Geneva event, which was also the 50th anniversary of the introduction of Jaguar's legendary XK120 sports car. The XKR shaved a second off the blown saloon's time to 60mph (96km/h), attaining this figure in the aforesaid 5.2 seconds, while the top speed remained the same.

Although outwardly resembling the XK8, the R, which is available in both open and closed forms, was easily identifiable by its bright mesh radiator grille. This provided a visual link with the XJR saloon that sports a similar feature.

When the blown 4 litre V8 engine was transferred to the sports car, adequate cooling became a major factor, so two louvred panels were set into the bonnet to let the hot air out. A red background to the Jaguar radiator badge, alloy wheels and a discreet rear lip were the only other identifying features.

The XKR is also enhanced by the presence of CATS, which stands for Computer Active Technology Suspension. As its name suggests, this provides electronically controlled adaptive damping, but the damper settings were also altered to make the car's handling even firmer.

Limited edition

To celebrate Jaguar's entry to Formula 1 in 2000, the company produced the limited edition XKR Silverstone with uprated suspension, enhanced interior and silver, rather than the usual gold, alloy wheels. The engine was unchanged; just as in the mainstream model, you might think that you were in a standard XK8, that is until you pressed hard on the accelerator…

Specification	Jaguar XKR
Engine location	Front, in-line
Configuration	Supercharged V8
Bore and stroke	86 x 86mm
Capacity	3996cc
Valve operation	Twin overhead camshafts per bank
Horsepower	370bhp @ 6150rpm
Transmission	Automatic five-speed
Drive	Rear
Chassis	Unitary
Suspension – front	Wishbones and coil spring
Suspension – rear	Wishbones and coil spring
Brakes	Ventilated disc
Top speed	Limited to 155mph (249km/h)
Acceleration	0-60mph (96km/h): 5.2 seconds

Mercedes-Benz CLK-GTR

Top speed
199mph
320km/h

Below: Awesome and purposeful, the radiator and headlamp treatment of the CLK-GTR was shared with the CLK coupé; this road-tamed racer even incorporates Mercedes-Benz's famous tri-star mascot. Although often regarded as a successor to the 300SL coupé of the 1950s, the doors are not of the gullwing variety although the car does possess a similarly high sill line.

With a price tag of £1.1 million, the CLK-GTR Mercedes-Benz of 1998 is not only the most expensive car in this book, it is still, at the time of writing, the company's fastest road car, being capable of 199mph (320km/h).

It is a spiritual successor to the fabled 300SL gullwing coupé of 1954-57, although it does not possess such memorable doors, using front-mounted scissor ones instead of gullwings. It was conceived as a roadgoing version of the company's racer which won the 1997 and 1998 GT championships. Homologation required that just one road car should be made, but Mercedes-Benz, which approved the project in March 1997, decided to build a 'small quantity' for private customers.

The first of the strictly two-seater coupés was delivered in November 1998 with the last of 25 examples being finished in the summer of 1999. Built in batches of three, each taking four to six weeks to complete, the work was undertaken by AMG at its factory at Ludwigsburg near Stuttgart. Since 1998 AMG had been Mercedes-Benz's in-

Racer tamed for the road

Built up around a carbon-fibre monocoque, the car's occupants could be in little doubt that this was a racer tamed for the road. Mounted longitudinally and directly attached to the rear bulkhead in the manner of the Ferrari F50, the 6.8 litre unit was based on the 5.9 litre V12 used in the S600 passenger models but developed by the UK-based Ilmor Engineering. Developing 612bhp with a massive 572lb/ft of torque, it raucously drove the

house performance arm. The car only differed in detail from the track-ready GTRs. The Kevlar bodyshell was reinforced, the suspension retuned to increase the ride height, and 18in (457mm) wheels were fitted. Inside there were sports seats, three-point safety belts, twin air bags and an integrated roll cage.

There were visual reminders of the newly introduced CLK coupé although these were confined to the radiator grille, the four headlamps and instrumentation.

rear wheels through a six-speed manual gearbox which was operated by twin paddles located behind the steering wheel. Unlike the similar unit used by Ferrari, the CLK-GTR was fitted with a clutch. Acceleration was astounding with 62mph (100km/h) arriving in just 3.8 seconds.

Interestingly, this latter day 'silver arrow' was diametrically opposed in concept to McLaren's celebrated F1 which featured racing technology in a car that was specifically designed for road use. This awesome Mercedes-Benz coupé was, by contrast, a racer tamed for the highway. In consequence, it was fitted with power steering, power brakes and traction control, all refinements that were noticeably absent from the F1.

Specification	Mercedes-Benz CLK-GTR
Engine location	Mid, in-line
Configuration	V12
Bore and stroke	89 x 92mm
Capacity	6898cc
Valve operation	Twin overhead camshafts per bank
Horsepower	612bhp @ 6800rpm
Transmission	Manual six-speed
Drive	Rear
Chassis	Carbon-fibre monocoque
Suspension – front	Wishbones, pullrod and coil spring
Suspension – rear	Wishbones, pullrod and coil spring
Brakes	Ventilated disc
Top speed	199mph (320km/h)
Acceleration	0-62mph (0-100km/h): 3.8 seconds

Above: Although it is not a particularly practical road car, the 'Silver Arrow' could not be anything but a Mercedes-Benz. The body panels are made of Kevlar and the rear spoiler is an essential aid to produce stability and downforce.

Left: The cockpit is a little congested although safety features abound with the presence of an integrated roll-over cage, and airbags for driver and passenger.

Aston Martin Le Mans Vantage

Top speed 200mph+ 322km/h

Right: Aston Martin banished the usual wood veneer in the Le Mans for titanium, a theme that echoed the Project Vantage concept car of 1998.

Below: The front of the Le Mans is noticeably different from the Vantage on which it was based. The nose and the bonnet and wing air intakes are all peculiar to the model.

Unashamedly purposeful and with a top speed in excess of 200mph (322km/h), this potent Aston Martin was able to hit 100mph (161km/h) in under 10 seconds. Little wonder that the supercharged V8 engine developed no less than 600bhp.

It represented the final expression of a line that began with the lacklustre Virage coupé of 1989. Since 1950 Aston Martin has applied the Vantage name to the most powerful model of its day and this Virage-based car was the flag-bearer developed for 1993.

The output of its 5.3 V8 engine was boosted from 310 to 550bhp, principally by the fitment of two Eaton superchargers. With a top speed approaching 190mph (306km/h), its brakes needed to be good and the 14in (356mm) diameter discs, courtesy of the corporate Group C racer, were the largest then fitted to a production car.

Three years on, in August 1995, a Mark II version of the model appeared that could be easily identified by a distinctive crackle-finished radiator grille. Beneath the surface no less than 700 modifications had been effected to refine handling, improve the gear change and reduce noise levels.

Then for 1998 came the top-of-the-range Vantage 600, the output of the venerable but robust V8 having been boosted to 600bhp, each blower now boasting its own intercooler. There was a new

five-speed gearbox, actually a Chevrolet Corvette ZR1 unit but with the top gear blanked off. Speeds in excess of 200mph (322km/h) were attainable.

Outward changes were minimal and discreet; for instance, the shape of the radiator grille was accentuated by a thin chrome surround. There was also a small but significant badge which declared *Works Prepared* and *Newport Pagnell* which is where this Aston Martin was built.

Anniversary of Le Mans victory

The 1999 Geneva Motor Show witnessed the arrival of the ultimate version, the Le Mans Vantage, which celebrated the 40th anniversary of Aston Martin winning the 1959 24 hour classic

event and the World Sports Car Championship. Available in 550 and 600bhp guises, the Le Mans was instantly identifiable by its reworked nose with enlarged radiator ducts in a new grille panel. It also incorporated an extended spoiler to aid downforce.

The range of colour schemes included the almond green paint of a hue used by the 1959 works team. Inside, the Le Mans revealed the influence of the interior of the Project Vantage concept car of the previous year. Just 40 cars, one for each year, were produced.

The last Le Mans off the line appeared at Aston Martin's stand at the 2000 British Motor Show, so allowing the V12-engined Vanquish to take centre stage in 2001.

Below: The number plate says it all! The Le Mans is based on the Vantage 600 which appeared in 1998. The thin chrome surround was a distinctive feature.

Bottom left: The Vantage engine. The output of the two Eaton superchargers, introduced in 1993, was boosted so that the V8 developed 600bhp. Each unit has its own intercooler and water pump.

Specification	Aston Martin Le Mans Vantage
Engine location	Front, in-line
Configuration	Twin supercharged V8
Bore and stroke	85 x 100mm
Capacity	5340cc
Valve operation	Twin overhead camshafts per bank
Horsepower	600bhp @ 6750rpm
Transmission	Manual six-speed
Drive	Rear
Chassis	Unitary
Suspension – front	Wishbones and coil spring
Suspension – rear	Wishbones and coil spring
Brakes	Ventilated disc
Top speed	Over 200mph (322km/h)
Acceleration	0-60mph (96km/h): 3.9 seconds

Chevrolet Corvette Z06

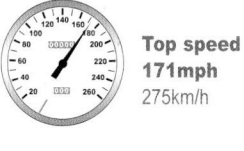

**Top speed
171mph**
275km/h

*Right: The Z06 name is
inspired by a special
Corvette Sting Ray of the
1960s although the hp
figure refers to the higher
American SAE rating.*

*Below: Based on the
Corvette Hardtop, the Z06's
styling changes include new
10-spoke alloy wheels, air
vents behind the front
wheels and mesh-covered
frontal air intakes.*

One hundred miles an hour (161km/h)
from standstill in less than a tyre-
scorching 10 seconds is just one of the
attributes of the Z06, the latest version of the
legendary Corvette, which was unveiled in 2000.

It was named in memory of the 1962 racing
Sting Ray coupé, of which only 199 examples were
built. But this latter-day version is rather more
plentiful and will account for about 20 per cent of
Corvette production. With annual output running at
some 33,000 cars, that's the equivalent of about
6500 examples per year.

The current Corvette shape appeared in 1997
and it is the fifth generation of a line that began
back in 1953. It had a glass-fibre body, just like the
original, and a full length perimeter seamless
tubular chassis lurked beneath those distinctive and
aerodynamically refined contours, which accounted
for an impressive 0.29 drag coefficient. A notable
feature was the fact that the all-independent
suspension was available with an active option.

Coupé and convertible models

Power was provided by a new LS1 all-alloy 345cid
(5.7 litre) V8 which developed 345bhp and drove
through a six-speed manual gearbox. Produced in
coupé and convertible forms, these were joined for
the 1999 season by a hardtop with detachable lift-
out roof panels. It is this latter version, which is
lighter than the coupé, that forms the basis of the
Z06. Outwardly similar to the mainstream 'Vette, it
can be identified by new ten-spoked alloy wheels
and discreet air intakes introduced in the front
spoiler and ahead of the rear wheels.

Left: This Corvette's lines are not interrupted by bumpers. The air vents in the rear apron are another feature peculiar to the Z06. The Eagle F1 tyres are specially developed by Goodyear, the wheels being one inch (25mm) wider than the originals.

Below: The new wheels with their forged alloy rims display the all-round ventilated discs to good effect; brakes are activated by a Bosch anti-lock system. The Corvette's petrol tank can hold 15 gallons (68lit) of fuel.

However, the real changes were to be found beneath the bonnet with the revised LS6 V8 now producing 385bhp. Improvements to harness the extra horses included high compression cylinder heads, redesigned inlet manifolding for better breathing, a 'hotter' camshaft and less restrictive titanium exhaust system.

Active-handling system

The already rigid suspension was also uprated with a new tauter rear springs; transverse front and rear, they are made from a composite material. The real secret of the Z06's roadholding is General Motors' second-generation active-handling system. Subtle and ingenious, its most significant feature is that it senses possible trouble ahead and the fuel supply and Bosch anti-lock disc brakes are unobtrusively trimmed accordingly. The driver, benefiting from supportive and distinctive red and black seats, will probably be unaware of its intervention!

Sure-footed, fast – it's capable of 171mph (275km/h) – and an uncompromising sports car, the Z06 is the latest manifestation of a line which, nearly 50 years on, shows itself to be as vibrant as ever.

Specification	Chevrolet Corvette Z06
Engine location	Front, in-line
Configuration	V8
Bore and stroke	3.9 x 3.6in (99 x 92mm)
Capacity	345cid (5654cc)
Valve operation	Pushrod
Horsepower	385bhp @ 6000rpm
Transmission	Manual six-speed
Drive	Rear
Chassis	Tubular steel
Suspension – front	Wishbones and transverse leaf spring
Suspension – rear	Wishbones and transverse leaf spring
Brakes	Ventilated discs
Top speed	171mph (275km/h)
Acceleration	0-60mph (0-96km/h): 4 seconds

Ferrari 550 Barchetta Pininfarina

Ferrari built a mere 448 examples of the 550 Barchetta Pininfarina, the open version of its 550 flagship coupé unveiled at the 2000 Paris Motor Show. Produced to commemorate the 70th anniversary of the creation of the famous Turin-based styling and coachbuilding establishment, it was priced at £172,000; wealthy collectors were said to be offering £30,000 above this asking price, even for second-hand examples.

After 23 years of producing mid-engined supercars, in 1996 Ferrari unveiled the 550 Maranello coupé with a front-located 485bhp 5.4 litre V12 engine. Capable of 199mph (320km/h), it is no surprise to find that it consumed petrol at a rate of 7.9mpg (35.5 litres/100km) for town driving, a figure that soared to around 18mpg (15.6 litres/100km) on long runs!

Originally the 550 was fitted with a six-speed manual gearbox which operated through the traditional Ferrari visible gate. However, from the 1998 season it became available with a Selespeed

automatic box which dispensed with the conventional clutch pedal. Borrowing technology from Ferrari's Formula 1 cars, gear changes were effected by two paddles mounted just behind the steering wheel rim.

Cloaked in a magnificently proportioned but understated Pininfarina body, this uncompromising two-seater boasted Ferrari's traditional tubular steel chassis, all-independent suspension and sophisticated ASR traction control.

Top speed 186mph 299km/h

Right: While the instrument panel is related to the 550 Maranello, the Barchetta's seats are new and are leather-trimmed carbon fibre. Competition-inclined owners can have a racing harness fitted.

Below: The Barchetta's nose is also 550-based, and the presence of an air intake is a reminder that this is a front-engined V12 Ferrari. The wheels are split-rim alloys.

After four years production, the coupé was joined in 2000 by the celebratory open-topped version. It was named the Barchetta in memory of Ferrari's first production car, the delectable Touring-bodied 166 open two-seater of 1948. Even more significantly it celebrated Pininfarina's foundation in 1930. First associated with Ferrari in 1952, and exclusively so since 1955, it is a partnership that continues to amaze and delight the motoring world.

No-frills barchetta concept

With a windscreen reduced by 3.9in (100mm) in height, the open 550 remains true to the no-frills barchetta concept by dispensing with a hood although a rudimentary cover is provided to protect the car's occupants in the event of sudden rain.

Twin roll-over bars feature at the rear with their contours echoed in the twin humped boot lid. Inside there are new carbon-fibre leather trimmed seats, with lucky customers being able to specify their own exterior colour and interior trim.

Although weighing about the same as the coupé (the lack of roof is offset by a reinforced body substructure), the Barchetta is slightly slower flat out than its stablemate, on account of the closed car's superior aerodynamics. It is thus capable of a mere 186mph (299km/h)!

Below: Classic lines: by the nature of its body, the Barchetta's windscreen is considerably shallower than that fitted to the 550M coupé.

Bottom left: Note that the retro-style twin fairings moulded into the boot cover echo the double roll-over hoops. The model comes complete with a rudimentary hood.

Specification	Ferrari 550 Barchetta Pininfarina
Engine location	Front, in-line
Configuration	V12
Bore and stroke	88 x 75mm
Capacity	5474cc
Valve operation	Twin overhead camshafts per bank
Horsepower	485bhp @ 7000rpm
Transmission	Automatic
Drive	Rear
Chassis	Tubular steel
Suspension – front	Wishbones and coil spring
Suspension – rear	Wishbones and coil spring
Brakes	Ventilated disc
Top speed	186mph (299km/h)
Acceleration	0-60mph (0-96km/h): 4.6 seconds

Bentley Continental T

The Continental coupé of 1991 had the distinction of being the first Bentley for 32 years to have its own purpose-designed bodywork. Hitherto, the magnificently appointed and refined saloons had been based on the products of its Rolls-Royce parent company. When this potent and luxurious grand tourer appeared, it signalled the emergence of Bentley as the dominant of the two marques after it had faced near extinction in the 1970s.

In 1982 the Bentley Mulsanne Turbo saloon had been unveiled. This was based on its Rolls-Royce Silver Spirit stablemate with the 6.7 litre V8 engine turbocharged to produce a 135mph (217km/h) car. It was followed, in 1985, by the better-handling Turbo R. Both models had the virtue of immediately attracting a new, affluent and, above all, youthful clientele which responded positively to a revival of Bentley's long dormant performance profile. In consequence, in 1990 Bentley production outnumbered Rolls-Royce output for the first time since the 1950s.

Bespoke body styling

The next step was a bespoke body which was the work of consulting stylists, John Heffernan and Ken Greenly. Their Project 90 concept coupé was displayed at the 1985 Geneva Motor Show and the public response was sufficiently encouraging for the company to proceed with the venture. The Continental R duly appeared six years later at the 1991 Geneva event.

Right: The T's special interior with engine-turned aluminium dashboard and centre console. Bentley's Personal Commission service enhances interiors to suit an individual buyer's own requirements.

Below: A Monaco Yellow Continental T for 2000. The model has a noticeably shorter wheelbase than the original. Great care is taken with the door furniture, the interiors of the handles being carefully knurled.

Based on the Turbo R's mechanicals, the model's name was a tribute to Bentley's legendary Continental of the 1951-59 era. The blown V8's output was boosted to 328bhp and this, along with the coupé's better aerodynamics, ensured that the model was able to carry a potential four passengers in considerable comfort at speeds of up to 150mph (241km/h). Bentley had been reborn.

Subsequently, at the 1996 Geneva show, the Crewe-based company unleashed the Continental T which it billed as the fastest Bentley yet. Wider, with a 4in (100mm) shorter wheelbase and lighter than the R on which it was based, engine output was increased to 400bhp. Capable of 170mph (274km/h) and able to reach 60mph (96km/h) in a mere 5.8 seconds, the T was also enhanced by a special interior with mottled aluminium dashboard, red starter button, micro-alloy disc brakes, revised suspension and electric traction control.

An even faster-accelerating variation on the theme appeared in 2000 with the Special Commission T, identifiable by its aerodynamically refined body lines. A further 20bhp was extracted from the venerable V8 by blueprinting the engine and adjusting the management system.

The seats were upholstered in quilted Connolly leather but there were only two of them. The rear ones were removed to leave space for bespoke matching leather luggage, fittings that were very reminiscent of the sporting Bentleys of the 1920s!

Specification	**Bentley** Continental T
Engine location	Front, in-line
Configuration	Turbocharged V8
Bore and stroke	104 x 91mm
Capacity	6750cc
Valve operation	Pushrod
Horsepower	400bhp @ 4000rpm
Transmission	Automatic four-speed
Drive	Rear
Chassis	Unitary
Suspension – front	Wishbones and coil spring
Suspension – rear	Semi-trailing arm and coil spring
Brakes	Ventilated disc
Top speed	170mph (274km/h)
Acceleration	0-60mph (0-96km/h): 5.8 seconds

Left: The visually enhanced appearance of the Bentley Continental T's venerable aluminium V8 engine, which dates back in essence to 1959. Less apparent is the presence of the Garrett turbocharger, Bosch Jetronic fuel injection and Zytek engine management system. An electronic traction system momentarily cuts back the engine if the wheels slip or spin.

Left: When a Continental T is on the move, and during spirited acceleration and cornering, the car's viscous control differential transfers power from a spinning wheel to one with traction. This is because of the substantial amount of power and torque, to the tune of 645lb/ft at 2100rpm, developed by the big V8.

BMW Z8

The latest recruit to BMW's fabled Z series sports car line, the Z8 clearly draws its visual inspiration from the company's classic 507 model of the 1950s. Produced between 1957 and 1959, the 507 was powered by a 3.2 litre V8 engine and could be wound up to 135mph (217Km/h). But it was expensive for its day and only 250 were produced. Now in demand by collectors, it fired the imagination of BMW's chairman and old car fan Bernd Pischetsreider and his fellow board member and classic car enthusiast Wolfgang Rietzle.

The result, the work of Henrik Fisker, the Danish head of BMW's California studio, was the Z8 concept car. It was unveiled at the 1997 Tokyo Motor Show. While some features of the concept car were sacrificed for the production line, the Z8, which appeared for the 2000 season, closely resembled the show version. But this was no pastiche of the original, it also incorporated a raft of 1960s features, courtesy of Austin-Healey, Jaguar and Aston Martin. However, the most

significant difference between the two cars is that the production version has been shorn of its D-Type-inspired rear fin. It has been replaced by more production-friendly twin roll-over hoops.

Aluminium space-frame

Aluminium featured extensively in the construction of the Z8, most significantly the space-frame that was welded and glued together, while the suspension components were made of the same

Right: The Z8's instrument panel contains retro elements. Moving the instruments to the centre of the dash means that the driver has an uninterrupted view down the bonnet.

Below: Inspired by BMW's 507 of the 1950s, with the wing-mounted side vents echoing that model, the Z8's structure makes extensive use of aluminium and is essentially a hand-made product.

Top speed
155mph*
249km/h
*Limited

metal. It therefore comes as no surprise to find that the body panels are also aluminium with the bumpers and boot lining made from strong and ultra-light carbon fibre. The Z8 weighs a very respectable 3494lb (1585kg).

It also perpetuated the spirit of the 507 in having a V8 engine, although this is a 5 litre unit developing an awesome 400bhp and comes courtesy of BMW's formidable M5 saloon. Under-bonnet warm air escapes through distinctive 507-style vents positioned on each side of the front wings.

Retro styling

There was a choice of a six-speed manual gearbox and an SMG sequential version of the same unit. Inside the retro themes were continued with a chrome-plate and leather-bound steering wheel. These went hand in hand with the latest gizmos, such as satellite navigation, a ten-speaker stereo and a hands-free mobile phone.

Although the Z8's top speed was limited to 155mph (249km/h), without this restriction it could probably attain 180mph (289km/h) and it can sprint to 62mph (100km/h) in just 4.7 seconds.

Unlike its much cheaper Z3 relative which is produced in America, the Z8 is assembled by hand in Germany. This is no mass-produced car; just ten a week are being built so this BMW will only be available for the fortunate few.

Above: The rear lights are distinctive and the twin exhaust pipes indicate a V8 engine. The back tyres are wider than the front ones.

Left: The model's 4.9 litre V8 engine is inherited essentially intact from BMW's potent M5 saloon. The Z8 is fitted with electronic stability and traction control.

Specification	BMW Z8
Engine location	Front, in-line
Configuration	V8
Bore and stroke	94 x 89mm
Capacity	4941cc
Valve operation	Twin overhead camshafts per bank
Horsepower	394bhp @ 6600rpm
Transmission	Manual six-speed
Drive	Rear
Chassis	Tubular aluminium
Suspension – front	MacPherson strut and coil spring
Suspension – rear	Multi link and coil spring
Brakes	Ventilated disc
Top speed	Limited to 155mph (249km/h)
Acceleration	0-62mph (0-100km/h): 4.7 seconds

Morgan Aero 8

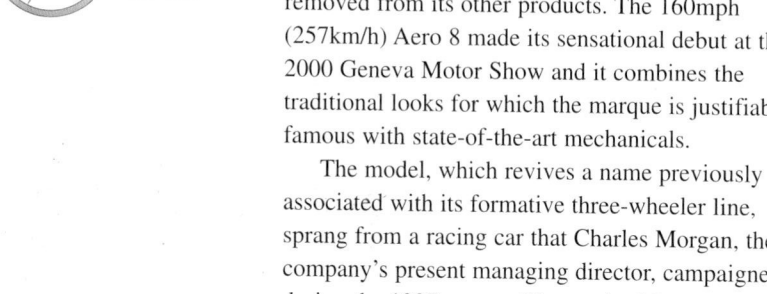

**Top speed
160mph**
257km/h

By any standards it is a sensational car, but for an old established company like Morgan it is positively light years removed from its other products. The 160mph (257km/h) Aero 8 made its sensational debut at the 2000 Geneva Motor Show and it combines the traditional looks for which the marque is justifiably famous with state-of-the-art mechanicals.

The model, which revives a name previously associated with its formative three-wheeler line, sprang from a racing car that Charles Morgan, the company's present managing director, campaigned during the 1997 season. The work of Jaguar's former engineering director, Jim Randle, and created for that year's GT championship, its chassis was constructed from laser-cut aluminium sections. These were then glued and bonded together in much the same way in which the Lotus Elise frame is constructed.

Hitherto every Morgan since the marque's foundation in 1910 featured sliding pillar independent front suspension. But the GT2 racer used an unrelated and distinctive all-independent system which has been inherited by the Aero 8. This uses long cantilever upper arms with lower wishbones at the front with long transverse rear wishbones and coil springs as the suspension medium. While the racer's chassis came up to scratch, its Rover V8 engine, based on the unit used to power the Plus 8, was beginning to show its years and rendered the car uncompetitive.

Morgan has made no such mistakes with its new road car and it is powered by BMW's current 286bhp 4.4 V8, as used in the 5-Series saloon, but of a unique specification to Morgan. The gearbox is also German and is a six-speed Getrag unit.

Controversial bodywork

Perhaps the most controversial aspect of the new car is its bodywork with the front headlight treatment producing raised eyebrows in some quarters. But at least this new Morgan cannot be mistaken for anything else! The lines of the open

Above: The aerodynamically refined front end gives the Aero 8 a personality all of its own. Power is courtesy of BMW and, unlike previous examples of the marque, all-independent suspension is employed.

Right: Benefiting from low weight and a combination of old and new themes, the Aero's alloy wheels are individually etched with the Morgan badge. They allow plenty of air to reach the all-round discs.

two-seater evoke some of the spirit of the traditional Morgans, but the Aero 8 only uses about a dozen parts, namely the hinges, bonnet latches and doors, in common with its contemporaries. However, it does retain the time-honoured ash frame used with an aluminium monocoque.

It may come as a surprise to discover that the Aero was wind tunnel-tested. The drag coefficient figure of 0.39 is not outstanding but it is a revelation in Morgan terms, and is 40 per cent lower than that achieved by the Plus 8 whose body lines are firmly rooted in the 1930s.

With a selling price of just under £50,000, some £16,500 more than the Plus 8, the Aero 8 represents a considerable gamble by Morgan which is one of Britain's few remaining indigenous car companies.

Above: The Aero's handling and performance have been praised, this being aided by the car's light weight.

Left: The new Morgan as it appeared at the 2000 British Motor Show. Access to the car is good, thanks to the long doors.

Below left: The interior similarly echoes old and new themes. The windscreen is electrically heated and the ash frame, rather than being concealed by trim, is exposed.

Specification	Morgan Aero 8
Engine location	Front, in-line
Configuration	V8
Bore and stroke	82 x 92mm
Capacity	4398cc
Valve operation	Twin overhead camshafts per bank
Horsepower	286bhp @ 5500rpm
Transmission	Manual six-speed
Drive	Rear
Chassis	Aluminium monocoque
Suspension – front	Cantilever, wishbones and coil spring
Suspension – rear	Wishbones and coil spring
Brakes	Ventilated disc
Top speed	160mph (257km/h)
Acceleration	0-60mph (0-96km/h): 4.7 seconds

TVR Cerbera Speed 12

The Speed 12 power unit

TVR has been producing its own engines since 1996 and the Speed 12 power unit consists of two twin-cam 24-valve cylinder blocks from the company's Tuscan Speed Six model mounted at 90 degrees to one another on a common crankcase. A 60 degree angle is far more common for Vee

This big Cerbera's starting point was the sports-racing Speed 12 that TVR exhibited at the 1996 British Motor Show. It was sidelined late in 1999 when the GT1 class for which it had been designed was discontinued. However, it was revamped for GT2 competition in 2000 and is also destined for road use as 'a race car with number plates'.

Unveiled at the Croft circuit, near Newcastle, in April 2000, the mighty 7.7 litre V12 engine was displayed in a detuned format and developed a mere 800bhp. It is hoped to have this version in production by late in 2002.

Some members of the exclusive 200mph-plus (322+km/h) club rely on subtlety to achieve their ends. No one could accuse TVR of adopting this approach with the Speed 12. With an anticipated 800bhp under its massive bonnet, it is attempting to wrest the mantle of the world's fastest car away from the McLaren F1.

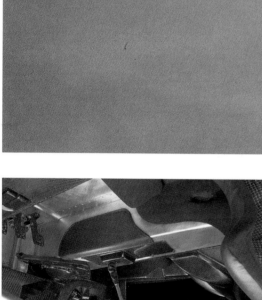

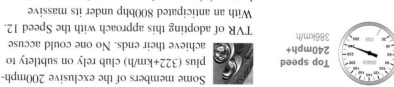

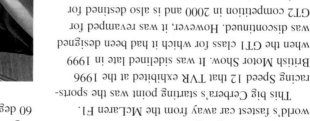

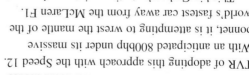
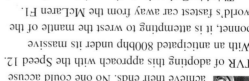
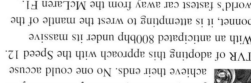

Top speed
240mph+
386km/h

Right: The Speed 12 readily betrays its racing origins, with the cabin featuring a minimalist approach – the emphasis is firmly on weight-saving.

Below: The Cerbera's body is made of carbon fibre. The twin exhaust pipes emerge ahead of the rear wheels on both sides.

engines so the resulting power unit is much wider than the norm and is mounted lower in the chassis.

Drive is taken through a six-speed Hollinger sequential gearbox and while the competition Speed 12 uses an automatic clutch, its roadgoing half brother has a conventional manual one.

Double wishbone suspension is employed all round and incorporates coil springs and pushrod-operated dampers. The brakes are massive AP racing ventilated discs at the front, arrested by no less than six piston calipers, with slightly smaller units at the rear. The stupendous horsepower developed by the V12 means that the massive 18in (457mm) diameter Speedline alloy wheels are wider at the rear than at the front.

With a chassis made of tubular steel and an aluminium honeycomb, the massive, audacious coupé body of the TVR flagship is made from carbon fibre with a large spoiler fitted at the rear to provide downforce and stability. The interior is austere with the accent on weight-saving; the instruments are grouped in a semi-circle around the steering column.

McLaren beater?

Only time will tell whether TVR's chairman, Peter Wheeler, will achieve his ambition of toppling the hi-tech McLaren from its perch. But bearing in mind TVR's extraordinary renaissance in recent years, the Blackpool-based company's bid deserves serious consideration.

Below: The TVR flagship on the move. The car, says its maker, is for 'racing drivers, not rich kids' who will drive to the circuit, compete in a race and then return home in it.

Specification	**TVR** Cerbera Speed 12
Engine location	Front, in-line
Configuration	V12
Bore and stroke	96 x 89mm
Capacity	7736cc
Valve operation	Twin overhead camshafts per bank
Horsepower	800bhp @ 7250rpm
Transmission	Sequential six-speed
Drive	Rear
Chassis	Tubular steel and aluminium honeycomb
Suspension – front	Wishbones, pushrod and coil spring
Suspension – rear	Wishbones, pushrod and coil spring
Brakes	Ventilated disc
Top speed	240mph (386km/h) (projected)
Acceleration	N/A

Porsche GT2

Capable of 196mph (315km/h), Porsche's twin turbocharged GT2 is the fastest road car in the company's history. Production has been restricted to just 300 examples. Launched at the 2001 Detroit Motor Show, it boasts a higher flat-out speed than its four-wheel-drive Turbo stablemate. Drawing on two variations on the 911 theme, its lightweight rear-wheel-drive chassis came courtesy of Porsche's no-frills competition-honed limited edition GT3 road car of 1999. The power unit was the latest water-cooled 3.6 litre version of the 911 Turbo engine which was boosted by 36bhp.

At 3175lb (1440kg), the GT2 weighed a significant 485lb (220kg) less than the current Turbo. While the absence of four-wheel drive accounted for some of this weight-saving, it also reflected the lack of rear seats, the electric activation of the front ones and an air conditioning system. This figure included a 35lb (16kg) saving from an unexpected quarter because the GT2 is the first production car to be fitted with race-bred carbon ceramic brakes. They had the virtue of not

Top speed 196mph 315km/h

Instantly identifiable

Outwardly the GT2 was modified to improve brake cooling and engine ventilation. It is instantly identifiable by the substantial air intakes incorporated in the front spoiler to cool the 13.8in (350mm) discs – the ducts mounted ahead of each rear wheel arch perform the same function. Greater downforce is provided by a fixed rear spoiler. It also sits 0.7in

only improving the coupé's stopping power, but also its steering.

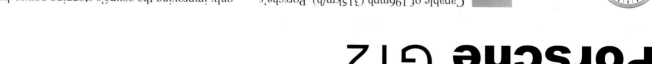

Right: The GT2's interior is functional and devoid of such weighty items as air conditioning and electric windows. The seats are comfortable and the driving position is excellent.

Below: The spoilered rear reveals that this is a far from ordinary 911 with a large air intake for the 3.6 litre flat-six engine and rear outlets for the heat generated by the adjacent ceramic discs.

(20mm) lower than the standard cars and uses wider tyres on larger 18in (457mm) alloy rims.

Although designed with competition in mind, the GT2 is a practical road car, although, as one overtakes you, any doubts about its identity will be banished by the presence of the name modestly adorning the back of the engine cover.

Power increase

Beneath it is the horizontally opposed six-cylinder GT3-based power unit with four valves per cylinder. It develops 456bhp rather than the Turbo's 420. This power increase was principally achieved by upping the boost pressure to the twin KKK K64 turbochargers. In addition, titanium connecting rods were fitted to permit the engine's revs to soar to an impressive 7900rpm.

However, while the GT2 can reach 62mph (100km/h) in an eye-blinking 4.1 seconds, the Turbo, on account of its four-wheel drive, is even more rapid and attains the same speed in four seconds. However, it forfeits 6mph (10km/h) flat-out speed to the lightweight Porsche, production of which ceased in 2001.

Above: The GT2 rides lower than the mainstream 911 with new wheels and tyres added to cope with the great increase in power. Further weight has been saved by not retaining the Turbo 911's four-wheel drive; only the GT2's rear wheels are driven. Created with track use in mind, just 300 examples were completed during 2001.

Specification	Porsche 911 GT2
Engine location	Rear, in-line
Configuration	Twin turbocharged horizontally opposed six-cylinder
Bore and stroke	100 x 76mm
Capacity	3600cc
Valve operation	Twin overhead camshafts per bank
Horsepower	456bhp @ 5700rpm
Transmission	Manual six-speed
Drive	Rear
Chassis	Unitary
Suspension – front	McPherson strut and coil spring
Suspension – rear	Multi link and coil spring
Brakes	Ceramic disc
Top speed	196mph (315km/h)
Acceleration	0-60mph (0-96km/h): 4.1 seconds

Aston Martin Vanquish

When, in 1997, stylist Ian Callum began work on the design of what was to become the Vanquish, he took a backward look as well as casting his eyes forward. As a result the company's new V12-engined coupé of 2001 is visually related to the legendary DB4 GT Zagato of 1960 vintage.

Born of a desire by Ford's DB4-owning president, Jac Nasser, to elevate Aston Martin, which Ford has owned since 1987, to the status Ferrari enjoys in Italy, this important corporate project is also intended as a showcase for the technological advances being made by the parent company. There is no shortage of them!

Project Vantage concept car

As a first step Nasser sanctioned the Project Vantage concept car which was launched at the 1998 Detroit Motor Show. And for all its retro elements, beneath the coupé's gleaming green-

painted aluminium panels was a state-of-the-art chassis. Receiving a rapturous reception from the public, Ford accordingly gave the project the green light and the result, some three years later, is the beautifully built Vanquish.

Unveiled at the 2001 Geneva Motor Show, the £158,000 model is outwardly almost identical to

Below: Immensely impressive, the Vanquish represents a formidable British challenger to Ferrari. Handling has won much praise.

Right: The cockpit perpetuates many of the themes displayed in Project Vantage. Gear changes are effected by using racing-style paddles behind the steering wheel.

Top speed 196mph
315km/h

the 1998 concept car although it is narrower by a mere 5.9in (151mm). The more obvious changes have taken place inside where detail alterations have been made to the dashboard, seats and controls. And there isn't a trace of wood veneer to be seen, just burnished aluminium. Available in a choice of styles, the Vanquish comes as an uncompromising two-seater or as a rather cramped two-plus-two.

Under the bonnet is a 5.9 litre V12 engine, with twin overhead camshaft and four valves per cylinder. It first appeared in 420bhp guise in the DB7 Vantage of 1999. Beginning life as two Ford Montego V6's mounted on a common crankcase, further enhancement and revision by in-house Cosworth has produced a 460bhp unit with a glorious exhaust note that is able to propel the Vanquish to a top speed of 196mph (315km/h) and push it to 60mph (96km/h) in 4.8 seconds.

Power is transmitted by a six-speed gearbox, which also functions in wholly automatic mode with the latest Formula 1-style paddle shift although it retains a clutch pedal. The all-independent suspension is by wishbones with braking the province of beautifully hand-finished, cross-drilled ventilated discs.

At the Vanquish's heart is a central aluminium tub with a carbon-fibre transmission tunnel and windscreen pillars made from the same material. The body structure is built up from aluminium extrusions that are bonded and riveted in place, while the outer panels are of the same material.

Aston Martin intends to produce 200 examples of its latest model in 2001 with numbers rising to 250/300 in 2002. Demand is likely to outstrip supply. Ferrari had better look to its laurels.

Above: One of the great appeals of the Vanquish is the exhaust note generated by the Cosworth-developed V12 engine. The 10J rear wheels possess excellent road-holding ability.

Left: The alloy V12 has been hailed as one of the outstanding aspects of the new Aston Martin Vanquish's specification. An underbonnet plate reveals the name of the individual who built this complex unit.

Specification	**Aston Martin** Vanquish
Engine location	Front, in-line
Configuration	V12
Bore and stroke	89 x 79mm
Capacity	5925cc
Valve operation	Twin overhead camshafts per bank
Horsepower	460bhp @ 6500rpm
Transmission	Manual six-speed
Drive	Rear
Chassis	Aluminium/carbon-fibre monocoque
Suspension – front	Wishbones and coil spring
Suspension – rear	Wishbones and coil spring
Brakes	Ventilated disc
Top speed	196mph (315km/h)
Acceleration	0-60mph (0-96km/h): 4.8 seconds

Index